Beloved . . .

Beloved . . .

the Memoir of Thelma Seheult

*T*HIS PERSONAL MEMOIR of Thelma Marie Camilla McDonald née Seheult was written by her while staying at the Riviera Beach Hotel Grande Anse, St. Georges, Grenada in 1972 and was typed by her daughter Robin Mc Donald.

Emily Seheult née Gray and her daughter Thelma age 4, in 1916.

*Our Memories Give Them Life
With Thanks And Love*

© 2016 Ian and Robin Mc Donald

All rights reserved. Except for use in review, no part of this publication may be reproduced or transmitted in any form or by any means, electronic or mechanical, including photocopy, recording, or any information storage or retrieval system, without permission in writing from the publishers.

Design and layout by Paria Publishing Company Limited
www.pariapublishing.com

ISBN: 978-976-8244-25-3
Typeset in Berling T
Printed by Lightning Source, USA

Contents

To my wife Thelma, a Tribute from her Husband   1

My Family   6
Tacarigua   26
Poole   34
Brasso   35
Siparia   37
My Encounter with Warrahoons   51
Tobago   57
Arima   75
St. Joseph   89
An Expedition to Mount St. Benedict   100
An Excerpt from my Diary   112
Christmas was a Time I Loved   116
St. Augustine   122
My Debut   125
Holiday in Barbados   128
The Sugar Revue   134
Archie   136
Our Wedding   146
Our Honeymoon   150
Bessie's House, Our First Home   154
Pregnancy   156
Birth of our First Baby   159
Boat Trip to Antigua   162
Antigua   165
Return Boat Trip to Trinidad   176
Arriving home   179
The Whitehead's House   182
Pregnant Again   187
Birth of our Second Child   190
Epilogue by her Children Robin and Ian McDonald   199
Notes   209

Thelma 1931

Archie 1931

To my Wife Thelma, a Tribute from her Husband

Who better should write an appreciation of a woman than her husband? One of her children perhaps? Our children have been as loving and affectionate as any parents could desire or expect and have given us a great deal of joy in our lives with only the normal amount of worry and trouble. But all children are apt to accept from their mother a whole lifetime of love and devotion as a matter of course, and they take for granted the day to day devotion and services as an accustomed part of their lives, until perhaps the day comes when these services are no longer available, and then when they themselves become parents, they realise the life time of self sacrifice, the sublimation of personal wishes and interests, and the fearless shouldering of responsibilities that are involved in motherhood.

But how can a man write about his beloved wife without embarrassment. After 34 years of happy married life, they have shared together joy and grief, happiness and despair, love and ecstasy, all the kaleidoscope of emotions that go to make up our human existence, and now they are like one person, knowing each others moods and faults and virtues and emotions and habit. And so for a man to write about his wife is to write about himself, their experiences together are personal to themselves and not to be laid bare for outside scrutiny, and yet my thoughts must be recorded now, as they may never be recorded.

Disagreements there must be in any human relationship, but when a man and woman have been fortunate enough to achieve a good marriage, their relationship becomes so precious to them that when tempers flare and quarrels raise their heads, each works consciously to repair the damage as soon as possible, lest each should lose that previous joy in one another that gives such meaning to their lives. How wrong they are who scoff at marriage.

A good marriage carries with it the true meaning and purpose and joy of life for every man and woman, and this has been my experience of marriage to the lady called Thelma Camilla Seheult.

My darling Thellie who in her youth was a beautiful and attractive girl; and in her maturity is a beautiful woman, and my lovely affectionate wife and devoted unselfish mother to our children. And now that we are both approaching the evening of our lives, she is still my darling companion and my lovely wife, and pray God that we may go on to the end of our days together.

To all outward appearances my own life in my teens and early twenties was happy and interesting, with all the usual activities of a schoolboy and a college student. I was, I suppose a fairly average young man, of average intelligence and ability, and good at games, so that I had many male companions. But during the youthful years of twelve to seventeen, I was at boarding school in England while my parents lived in the West Indies, so that I never saw my mother and father, or had the benefits of a real home during these adolescent years. I had no experience of mixing with young girls of my own age under normal home conditions during my school holidays. Perhaps for this reason, when I left school at the age of seventeen I was painfully shy in my social contacts, especially with members of the opposite sex, a shyness that was often mistaken by others for rudeness and stand-offishness, and which caused me to be awkward and reserved, particularly in mixed company. In order to boost my self confidence on social occasions I began to gulp down large quantities of alcohol, and began to take a peculiar pride in being able to drink at least on even terms with any of my companions, men of whom had far more capacity and far more robust constitutions than I had.

From my own personal experiences I can testify to the torment of uncertainty and even despair that such a man goes through in his early youth. From the time that he starts to grow out of childhood; and the sheltering love of his parents begins to cloy and even irritate, he strides out into the adult world full of dreams and ideals and ambitions that he is seldom able to realise. Nature begins to plague him with strange urges and emotions. His developing glands set fire to his body arousing a male aggressiveness and a torrent of sexual desire that in our modern civilisation can only be temporarily assuaged but cannot adequately be satisfied. Outside the shelter of his home he finds no friends, acquaintances by the score, yes, but no friends. Plenty of good companions on the playing field and the club house to slap him on the back and call him a fine fellow and urge him on to further wildness and extravagances that can earn the plaudits of the crowd; but that also undermines his moral fibre and makes him more and more desperate in his innermost self about ever finding any real purpose, or real interest or real happiness in life. He does not even know what he is looking for, what he is seeking from life.

There are the recurrent parties with the noise and false gaiety and the pretty attractive girls that only tease but cannot satisfy the torturing urges with which nature is tormenting him. There is the anesthetic haze of alcohol leading to hair breadth escapes that undermine his health and may even imperil his very life. And so he drifts on from one day to the other in an agony of purposeless indecision until one day, if he is lucky things are suddenly different, the sun seems to shine more brightly, the trees are greener, and his steps on the pathway of life are firmer and more decisive. He has met the one person who is different, the one person who can complement and stabilise his personality. This is not only sexual attraction, there is the indefinable feeling that this lovely girl is really on his side, she is really concerned for his welfare, she is not only attracted to him as a man, but really likes him as a person, and if need be would stand by his side against all the world to the end of time.

What a difference now in the pathway through life, he will hear that welcoming voice and see that welcoming smile and enjoy the exciting companionship of this special person and to go to bed at night knowing that tomorrow she will still be there and for all the tomorrows.

And then comes marriage and life now has a more certain direction. No work can be too hard, no problem too difficult, no disappointment too great, for sustaining such a man through all his waking hours in the certain knowledge that at the end of the day, there is a haven of rest and welcome, and joy and excitement awaiting him in his home. No longer are his youth and strength a torment, they are channeled and directed to the worthwhile tasks of life, and the very nature and meaning of sex has changed for him. No longer does he have the alternating torment and half-shameful ephemeral satisfaction of his youthful experiences. Now there is no joy on earth to compare with the fire and excitement of sex with a beloved partner. A fire and excitement that brings with it a lasting satisfaction and leaves an aftermath of warmth and tenderness, a lingering affection and loyalty for one another that gives a new meaning and a new purpose to all the everyday tasks and problems and difficulties of life. And when troubles come, as come they must, what steadfastness a man derives from a beloved wife, what never failing comfort and support. Sympathising and helping him in his weakness and praising and encouraging his strengths, always finding time from the multitudinous tasks of running a home, and looking after a family of six children, to give her man attention and companionship.

It is said that marriage is a gamble, and if this is so, then I have indeed been fortunate, for on looking back over my own life I am aware of starting to live more intensely, of finding a new purpose and a new meaning in life from the time that I knew that this lovely girl that I wanted more than anything on earth would love me and stand by me for always.

One sees around the world too many broken and unhappy marriages, and some marriages can in fact be a prison of despair from which one or both partners are longing to escape, and so I can count myself lucky and say a prayer of thanks that our marriage has been a happy one, and if one day my children or grandchildren should read these lines, they may serve to give them confidence and strength and assurance that marriage can indeed by the supreme and sustaining joy of life.

I pray that all my children and my childrens' children will have such loyal and beloved partners to walk beside them, at least a part of the way, along the difficult pathways of life.

I apologise to anyone reading these lines who may be embarrassed by this tribute, but I am now in my sixtieth year, we have been married for 34 years, and I wish to set down this record while I am still in full possession of my strength and health and mental faculties.

John Archie McDonald
31st January 1966

Beloved . . .

the Memoir of Thelma Seheult

Today is my birthday, I am 60 years old and it is a good day to start to write about my life from the time that I can remember.

I HAVE COME TO A CROSSROADS IN LIFE. We have just sold our house in Carmody Road, St. Augustine (with all our furniture) in which we lived so happily for 28 years. We are now marking time in Grenada, staying near to Gillie and Doug and our two little grandchildren, Cathy and Skene, and enjoying it, but in a way longing to once more have a place of our own with our things around us. After two years of wandering around like nomads it is time that we do so.

In the meantime, while I am here in Grenada, I have time to write—it is something for me to do and it may be of interest to my children and grandchildren, especially my grandchildren, to read of a completely different way of life to the one that they live now and will live in the future.

My Family

I was born at 2 o'clock on a Saturday afternoon on the 31st August, 1912, at a place called "Paradise House" in the ward of Tacarigua, Trinidad W.I. My father was Leo Gabriel Seheult and my mother was Emily Norah Gray, always called Emmie. My father was a qualified civil engineer with very good degrees from London & Edinburgh Universities. He won a scholarship at St. Mary's College for the best math scholar in Trinidad and this enabled him to go away and study,

*My mother Emily Norah Clarita
Gray as a young woman.*

as his family was not very wealthy and in those days only wealthy people sent their children abroad to be educated or qualified.

My father's grandfather was Jean-Jacques Seheult, who had came out to Trinidad as French Consul. I will not go into his ancestry, as my husband has that written down in a family tree that he compiled very carefully (*note 1*). However, I will mention my father's brothers and sisters, as while I am writing of my childhood I will probably often mention them and it will be easier to know who is who.

The eldest in my father's family was Henri Seheult, then Aimée (she married a Urich, of German ancestry), then my father, then Eugenie Seheult (also called Jenny, she married Frank Maingot), then Robert, then Rosemary (she married her first cousin Freddie Seheult) and last of all André, always called 'Popo' which was patois for baby. My father's father was Louis Adhemar Seheult. His wife died soon after André was born, and when my father and all his brothers and sisters were still young, they were brought up by their grandmother who was very bigoted and thought that once they went to church every day that was all they needed. As a result, all the children suffered from lack of a mother's love in their life.

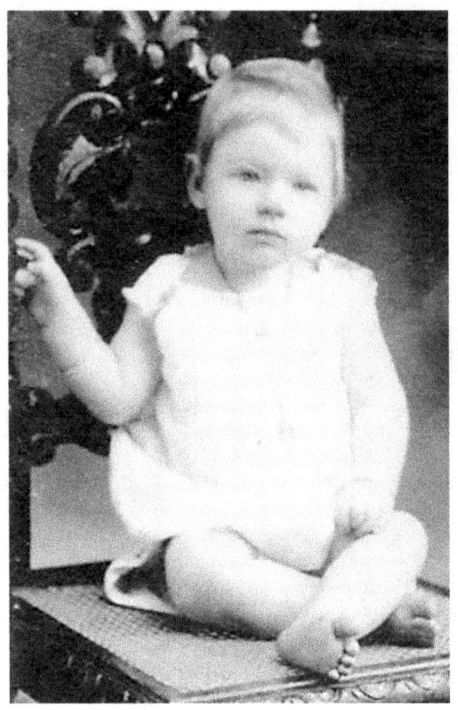

Me at 8 months (1913)

I was taken by my mother and father as a small child to visit my great-grandmother on my father's side. I remember her very distinctly as a very little person, all dressed in black and most forbidding. When I spoke to her she garbled something to me, which I could not understand but which I afterwards knew was French and then turned to my mother and garbled something fiercely to her. I could see my father getting upset and mother also. On our way home I realised that she had been angry with my mother because she wasn't speaking French, saying that she could not speak English. This, my father said, was untrue as she spoke and understood English very well, it was just that she wanted to be difficult. I was very small and don't remember all that was said, but I know my father was angry and my mother unhappy. I don't remember ever visiting 'Me-me' (that is what her grandchildren called her) again and I certainly never missed it.

My mother was the second daughter of Norah and William Gray. My maternal grandfather was a very quiet and gentle old man and my mother was the apple of his eye. She was good to him and she could do no wrong in his sight.

My maternal grandmother was a woman of great character and charm of manner. She was witty and amusing and everyone loved her; she was the strong one of the family and my grandfather was much too soft and indecisive for her. I don't think my grandmother ever really loved my grandfather, it was one of those matches made in the olden days. First of all, he was much older than her and was a magistrate in one of the country districts which my grandmother didn't like at all. I was small and didn't understand these things at the time, but as I got older I realised that my grandmother never loved my grandfather and he was very much in love with her.

My mother had an elder sister called Muriel who married Jack Evans. We never called her Aunt Muriel because she insisted that all her nieces and nephews call her Auntie (in a very English accent). She never had any children of her own and loved all her nieces very much though she was always correcting us and teaching us good manners and trying to make us speak in an English accent.

We were all a bit frightened of her when we were small, but when we got older realised she only corrected us because she loved us and wanted us to be very elegant and well mannered.

Leo Seheult, my father.

Uncle Jack Evans was an Englishman. His family had come out to Tobago to run an estate—I never knew which it was—but instead of running the estate, he took to drinking very heavily and as long as I knew him he never worked, depending completely on his family to send him money. He had been in the cavalry during the Boer War and often told us stories of the Boers and all the things they did, like pretending one of their family had died and taking the coffin out and having a burial, only for the English to discover long after that no one had died and the coffins were filled with arms and ammunition.

He told us many other stories of South Africa, what a beautiful country it was, but spoilt by the Boers who he really thought were horrible people—I expect he only saw one side of the picture. Uncle Jack was a very brave man and could suffer the worst pain without a murmur. He was devoted to Aunt Muriel, who although she was kind to Uncle Jack, as far as I knew never really loved him. The reason she married him I will never fathom as she was a very beautiful woman and had many admirers.

Louise de Maury de Lapeyrouse

My mother said she married Uncle Jack on the rebound from a broken love affair with an officer called Curran, whom she loved very much and who went away and then wrote to say he could not marry her and could not tell the reason why. When I was a young girl, she often told me about Curran, whom she had loved so much. Poor old Uncle Jack, I expect the fact that Aunt Muriel never truly loved him didn't help him to cut down on his drinking.

On the other hand I felt sorry for Aunt Muriel, too, who must have been very unhappy being married to Uncle Jack who never worked and drank so heavily. Thinking back I often wonder how she stood the life she had. I think of myself so happily married, with a husband who loves me very much and whom I love so very much after 40 years of marriage, and I wonder how I would have acted under the conditions that she had to live. She never had a home of her own; she always lived with my grandmother and grandfather, and my great-aunt Anna Collins, my grandmother's sister, and Uncle Harry Collins, their brother. I also wonder how Jack was able to live under those conditions. I never heard him lose his temper with any of the family and he was always a perfect gentleman, but he did make poor Auntie see misery. I do think (now that I can understand these things better) it was because he knew Auntie never loved him and this hurt him deeply.

Uncle Willie was my mother's older brother. I didn't know him very well but I remember him as a silent, shy, weak sort of man. He married a Venezuelan girl, I can't remember her second name and I only knew her as Aunt Lottie. There was a great to do over their marriage and no one spoke to Uncle Willie and Aunt Lottie, they were not accepted. Then Ena, their eldest child, was born and Uncle Willie brought her to show her to grandma and grandpa, and of course there was a great reconciliation and everything was forgotten and forgiven and Ena was always grandma and grandpa's favourite grandchild. She spent more time with my grandmother than she did at her own home. Uncle Willie and Aunt Lottie had lots more children; they came regularly, first Ena, then Joy, then Alan, then Phyllis, then Corie, then Flynn, then Ethine, then Joan. There was always a crisis when a new baby was on the way, as Uncle Willie had a very small job (at the Customs I think) and they always ended up on my grandmother's doorstep. How they all survived and got enough to eat and clothes to wear, I often wondered, but they did. Aunt Lottie had a sister who had married a wealthy doctor called Camps and I think she helped them quite a lot too.

Louis Adhemar Seheult

The Grays, Ena, Joy etc. played a big part in my life as a child as there was always one or two of them spending time with me and they were more like sisters than cousins. Then there was Uncle Gus, he married Edith Daly and had two sons, Broderick and Gordon. Uncle Gus was quite different to Uncle Willie, good-looking, full of charm and very sure of himself. Gus was always an attractive personality and full of fun and wit, but he liked the ladies and liked the drink more than was good for him.

I can't go on with the family background without mentioning Aunt Anna Collins. She never married, but she was the mainstay of the family. She sewed beautifully and made quite a lot of money making hats for rich ladies and sewing the most exquisite baby clothes and making dresses for the whole family. She was my godmother and no one ever had a better godmother. She made all my dresses, nightgowns and rompers (a sort of play-suit with little puffed pants). No little girl was better dressed than I was. She also spent lots of her precious time making lovely dolls clothes for my dolls, and if anyone in the family was ill, Aunt Anna was always called upon to go to nurse them.

She was a wonderful woman, who hadn't much in her life, but she had a very full and meaningful one and was never idle. What the rest of the family would

Aunt Anna Collins, Uncle Jack Evans, Aunt Muriel Evans 1900s

have done without her I don't know. I know that she was a second mother to me, and even when I got married, she made all my babies' clothes and often stayed with me if I wasn't feeling too well. Anyway, she will figure very much in my story of my memories of the past.

Uncle Harry Collins was also a very big part of my childhood memories, as he always lived with the family. He never got married, he never had enough money, yet he always helped support Aunt Anna and his old mother when she was alive.

Well, these are the people who were very much part of my childhood and now that I have given the background of both sides of my family, my father's and my mother's, I will begin to relate all the things and times that I can remember from my earliest years.

Norah Collins Gray, my grandmother, and William St. Clair Gray, my grandfather

Norah as a young woman

Jack Evans, Muriel Gray's husband

Left: Aunt Muriel

Text in the autograph book below reads:
Dark is her hair, her hand is white
Her voice is exquisitely tender.
Her eyes are full of liquid light
I never saw a waist so slender.
A little tiny pretty witty charming darling is she!
To love her was a liberal education
I like the "... chariot" -wheels are curves
Still to be near but never to be first.

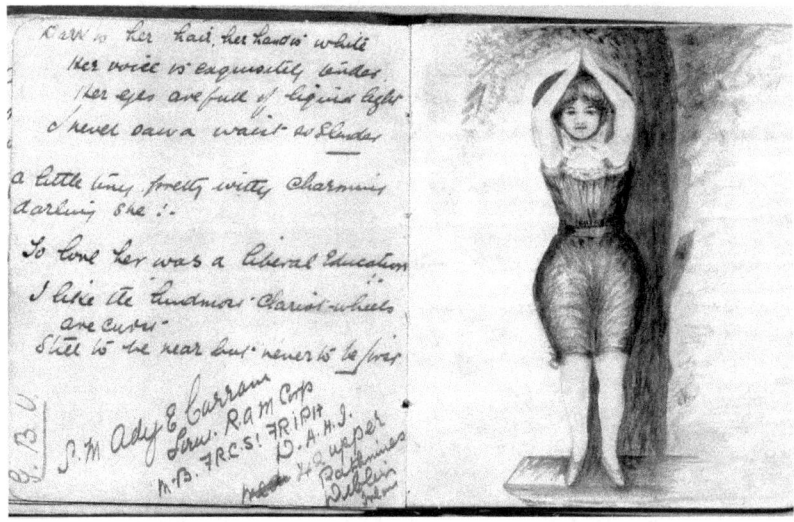

Note from Curran with a saucy drawing found in Aunt Muriel's autograph book dated 1901.

Five sons of Adhemar Seheult:
Robert, André, Henri, Leo and Joseph

Advice to Girls

Put not your trust in man
Not even in a brother
Girls if you must love
Love one another

— — —

Put not your trust in man
Not even in a brother
Girls if you must love
Love some one else brother

Willie Gray

Trinidad

With a fair coral strand up rises the land
  From the blue Western Sea's placid breast
And to write, 'tis a duty, in praise of the beauty
  Adorning this "Isle of the Blest".

In this wonderful spot, it's infernally hot
  'Tis a truth that can not be suppressed
But with beauty it's teeming, a fact quite redeeming
  The heat in the "Isle of the Blest".

In a tropical clime, it's not easy to rhyme
  And the sun quite annihilates zest
So wish in conclusion another intrusion
  Ere long, on the "Isle of the Blest".

Introduced by
H.S. Talbot.
11.2.98

Queen's Park Hôtel

TRINIDAD B.W.I.

Port of Spain *12th Feb., 1905.*

DINNER.

Hors D'Oeuvre.
Oysters.

Soup.
Soup à la Mikado.

Fish.
Baked Snapper à la Parisienne.

Entrées.
Pasteten.
Sauerbraten Mit Kartoffel Klössen.

Joints.
Boiled Ham.   String Beans.
Roast Beef—Brown Gravy.
Roast Turkey—Stuffed.

Vegetables.
Windsor, au Gratin & Boiled Potatoes.
Baked Yam.   Egg Plant.   Sugar Corn.

Sweets
Plum Pudding.
Ice Cream.   Cakes.
Cheese.
Coffee.

Franklin's Electric Printery.

JOHN McEWEN
Manager.

Above: A menu and drawing of The Queen's Park Hotel 1905 with a truly international menu.
Opposite top: 'Advice to girls' by Willie Gray, my grandfather.
Opposite bottom: A verse called 'Trinidad' by Captain Woodman of the HMS Talbot dated 1898. These poems were found in old autograph books.

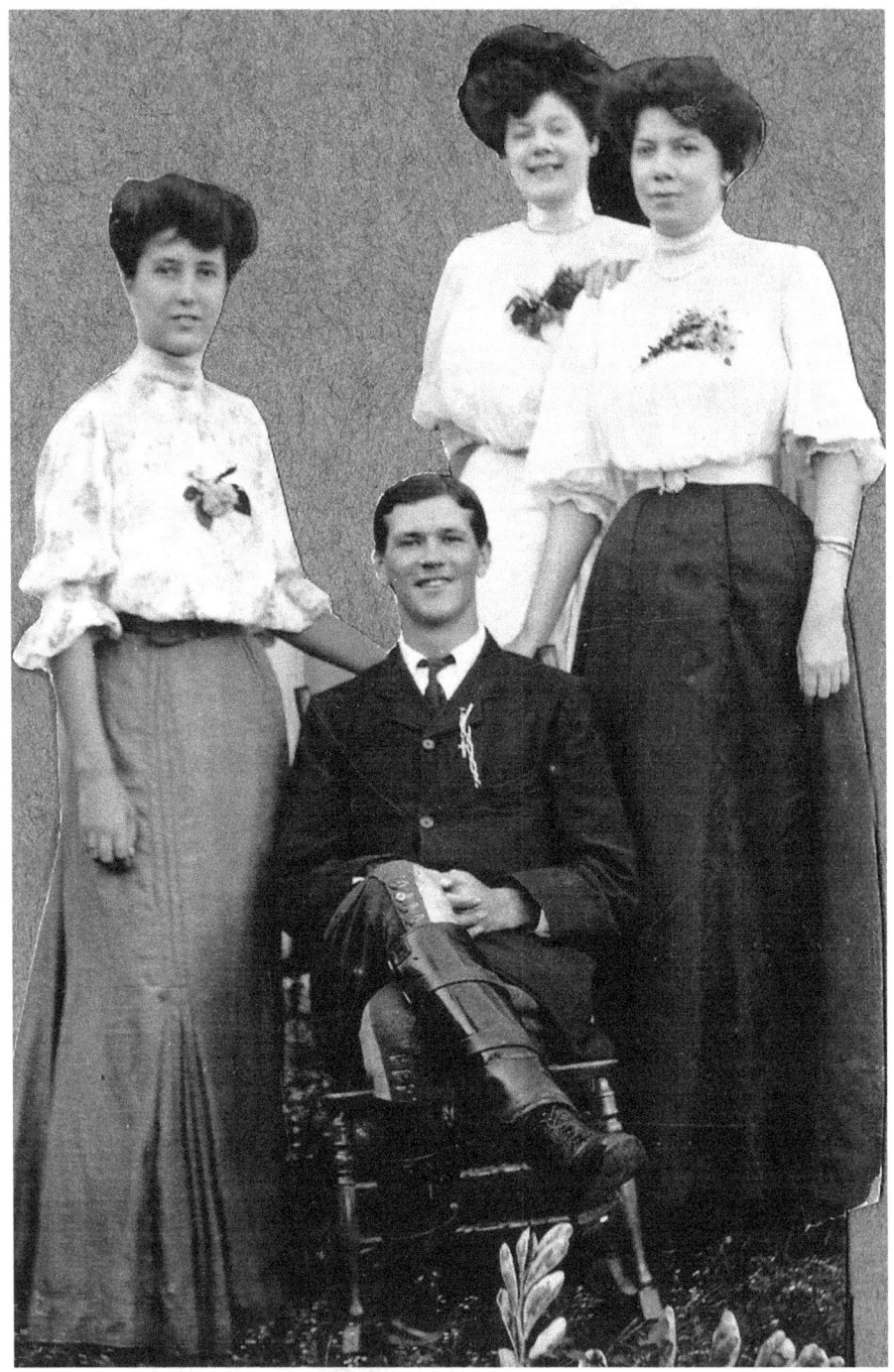

Emily Gray with Muriel Gray, Gus Gray and Anna Collins

Jenny Seheult (my father's sister) and her husband Frank Maingot with their children Joan and Ken.

Jenny and Joan

Joan & Ken Maingot

Family of Adhemar Seheult

Bertha Seheult née Maingot, Fernand Jacques Seheult, Henri Seheult and Rose May Seheult

Ena Gray, Norah Collins Gray, Emily Gray Seheult, me, Mr. and Mrs. Rooks, Leo Seheult (1914)

Cecile Seheult, Vicente de Montbrun, Marie Seheult, Anna Seheult, Losea Seheult, Leon Seheult, Estelle (Stella) Seheult, Marie Mimi Seheult née Girod, mother Girod, Felix Seheult, Raoul Seheult

Willie Gray Family: Lottie, Ena, Joy, William, Phyllis, Cora, Ethne and others.

Uncle Jack Evans (Muriel Gray's husband) and family, taken in the garden at "Capri", 24 July 1917. The gentleman on the left looks like Aucher Warner.

Family Tree: Seheults, De Lapeyrouse, Condon and Gray

Jacques Alexis de Verteuil	mar.	Josephe, Marie, Dupont, de Vivier, de Gourville 1795
Julien Michel de Verteuil	mar.	Jeanne Legendre de la Bretagne 1820
Losia de Verteuil	mar.	Jean Jacques Seheult 1850
*Adhemar Seheult	mar.	Louise de Maury de Lapeyrouse 1880
Leo Gabriel Seheult	mar.	Emily Gray 1911
Thelma Camilla Seheult	mar.	John Archibald McDonald 1932

Ian. 1933   Heather 1935   Gillian 1939   Robin 1943   Monica 1945   Archie 1952

Louis de Maury de Lapeyrouse	mar.	Anne de Cassiere 1785
Louis Michel de Maury de Lapeyrouse	mar.	Jeanne Eugenie de Masse 1820
Louis de Maury de Lapeyrouse	mar.	+Rose Condon 1850
Louise de Maury de Lapeyrouse	mar.	*Adhemar Seheult 1880

Francois Thomas Dabadie	mar.	Louise Adelaide Fancoise Peschier 1790
Marie Rose Dabadie	mar.	Jean Butler Condon 1820
+ Rose Condon	mar.	Louis de Maury de Lapeyrouse 1850

Alexander Robert Gray (Born in Lanarkshire, Scotland about 1825)	mar.	Emily Francis Webster 1855
William Gray	mar.	Norah Collins 1880
Emily Gray	mar.	Leo Gabriel Seheult 1911
Thelma Camilla Seheult	mar.	John Archibald McDonald 1932

Ian 1933   Heather 1935   Gillian 1939   Robin 1943   Monica 1945   Archie 1952

Adhemar Seheult clan
My father Leo sitting on last step

André Seheult—Leo Seheult's youngest brother

* * *

WE regret to record the death of *André Seheult* popularly known as 'Popo,' youngest son of the late Mr. Milhemar Seheult, on the 30th December, 1941.

He was educated at St. Mary's College and represented his college at soccer for several years as a brilliant centre half. He was a great favourite with the crowd, who never failed to appreciate the cleverness and cleanness of his play.

On leaving College he took to Agriculture, and was recognised as a very capable and progressive cocoa planter. Later, he received an important appointment on the staff of the United Fruit Company in Panama, which he held until the outbreak of war in 1914, when he volunteered for service overseas. He was among the first to leave for England as a member of the 1st Merchants' Contingent.

He served throughout the Great War in France, Belgium and Italy and returned to Trinidad in August, 1919.

His comrades in the King Edward's Horse, in which regiment he served right through the War, looked upon him as a particularly daring and fearless soldier. On the day of the armistice whilst pursuing the Boche at Ath in Belgium, he advanced so far alone that he was taken for a German and fired on by his own men.

On his return from the Front, he resumed his interest in Agriculture and later took up an appointment as Labour Superintendent in a large American Oil Company in Venezuela.

"Popo" was of a very happy and jovial disposition, which won him a host of friends, who were shocked to hear of his death.

R. E. P.

Tacarigua

Emily Seheult with me (1914)

As I mentioned at the beginning of my recollections, I was born at "Paradise House" (what a lovely name) in the Ward of Tacarigua in Trinidad, in those days the British West Indies.

I can't remember the house as my father and mother left there when I was about one year old. However, my mother has often spoken to me of the house and its lovely spacious rooms with big Demerara windows and pitch pine floors, scrubbed shining white with sour orange slices that were put in the water. The floors had a silvery sheen and the multi-coloured rugs on the floor and the white voile curtains at the windows, blowing in the breeze, has often been related to me. Years after, when I was married and lived in St. Augustine, I got my husband to drive me to Tacarigua and we had a look at the house I was born in.

It looked shabby, but it was a gracious old house with a wide verandah all around, a beautiful samaan tree like a huge green umbrella to the west of the house and a lovely pink poui in full bloom. Even though it was shabby and needed a coat of paint, it was a house of charm and character, and I wonder if it is still there or has been knocked down to make room for a square of concrete. Well, what to do, things change, but I can't say very often for the better.

My mother and father were very happy there and I have often heard my mother say that was her little bit of paradise on earth. From "Paradise House" they moved to another big old rambling house called "Laurel Hill", this was also in Tacarigua and not very far from Paradise House. My father, who had joined the railways on his return to Trinidad from university, and got the princely sum of $120.00 per month, was promoted in charge of roads and bridges in that area and now received $125.00 per month! They had a horse and buggy and a groom to look after the horse. They paid $15.00 a month rent, the groom $10.00 per month, the cook $3.00, the nurse $3.00, and the maid and washer $3.00.

There was also the yard boy, a young Barbadian lad called Thorington, but we always called him 'Carrington' (*note 2*). He came to work for my father at the age of 14 years, cleaning the yard, cleaning shoes, cleaning silver and brass, and doing all the odd jobs about the house and garden. He stayed with our family until my father died in 1939. My mother was left very badly off, she just had daddy's pension and the house which hadn't been paid for, so she couldn't keep on Carrington. Murray O'Neil in the Public Works Department gave him a job driving for the Public Works. He wasn't at all happy there, but I am glad to say that he got a very good job as chauffeur for the manager of Shell Leaseholds driving his private car, and he was very happy and well paid in this job. After a time we lost touch with him, I am sad to say, as he had always been very much a part of my life. I expect it was a lot of my fault. I was so engrossed with my own affairs, my husband and my growing family and also with my mother, grandmother, Aunt Anna and Aunt Muriel, that I didn't seem to have much time or energy for anything else, and one really can't do everything in life. If I had tried to keep in touch with all the old help and family retainers, I think my own family would have been neglected as I just hadn't the time or surplus energy to deal with all and sundry.

Me aged 4 (1916)

To go back to the time at "Laurel Hill" my mother said by the time they had paid rent, servants, and food for the horse, there wasn't very much surplus left and there was always someone in the family, either on my father's or mother's side, who needed a helping hand. I wonder what the young couples of today would think of that way of life. They need all the luxuries of life from the day they get married.

My mother said she had one pair of shoes, which did for all occasions, and a pair of leather slippers that she wore in the house. They were all made by local shoemakers, as the imported shoes were very expensive and only the rich people could afford those. She had one good skirt and two pretty blouses, made of the finest linen with tiny pin tucks and Valenciennes lace (*note 3*). Aunt Anna made these and they were a work of art. These were worn for all occasions and she had two little gingham gowns that she wore during the day in the house.

My mother said she was very happy and content and felt she had all that she could have wished for, a husband she loved, a lovely baby (me!), a lovely house and peace and quiet. She often saw her family—my grandfather loved to come to spend a week or two with my parents, he got on well with my father. In the afternoons, they would all walk in the garden and along the long driveway, which was bordered with beautiful samaan trees that made a lacy canopy overhead.

OLD SONG

I

I was strolling one day
Down the Royal Arcade
The place for childrens toys
Where you may purchase
 A dolly or a spade
For good little girls and boys.

II

And as we passed a certain stall
Said a little wee voice to me
"Oh! I'm a Colonel in a little cocked hat,
And I ride on a tin gee-gee."
"Oh! I'm a Colonel in a little cocked hat,
and I ride on a tin gee-gee."

III

"There's a pretty little dolly girl over there,
And I'm mad in love with she,
and oh! she's dressed in a beautiful dress,

It's a dress I do admire
And once in a while
When the folks were gone
She used to flirt with me,
But now that I'm only marked
 one e nine (1/9)
She turns up her nose at me
She turns up her little pug nose at me,
and flirts with two e three (2/3)".

IV

"Cheer up oh little tin Man" said I
"I'll see what I can do"
So I took down the label marked 1/9
 e labelled him two and three
I felt so sorry for that little tin man
As he rode on his tin gee-gee.
I felt so sorry for that little tin man
As he rode on his tin gee-gee ♡♡♡

A SONG/POEM GRANDMA EMMY SEHEULT USED TO SING TO HER DAUGHTER THELMA & IN TURN MUM SANG IT ETC TO US.

Song recorded by Thelma's daughter Gillian Howie née McDonald
in conversation with her mother

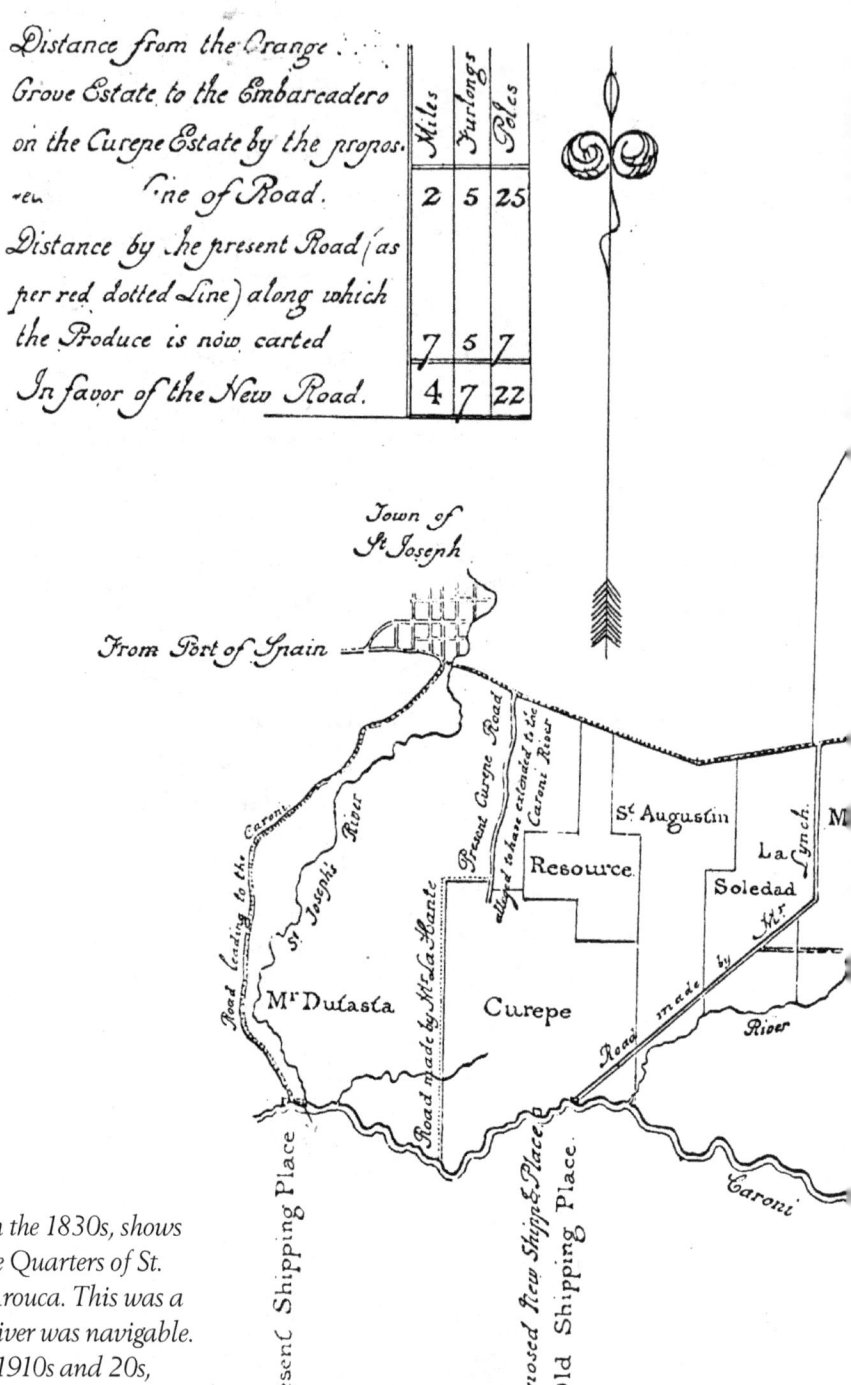

This plan, dating from the 1830s, shows the cane estates of the Quarters of St. Joseph, Tacarigua & Arouca. This was a time when the Caroni river was navigable. Growing up in the 1910s and 20s, Thelma would have been familiar with these estates, living in houses at St. Joseph, St. Augustine, Paradise and Laurel Hill.

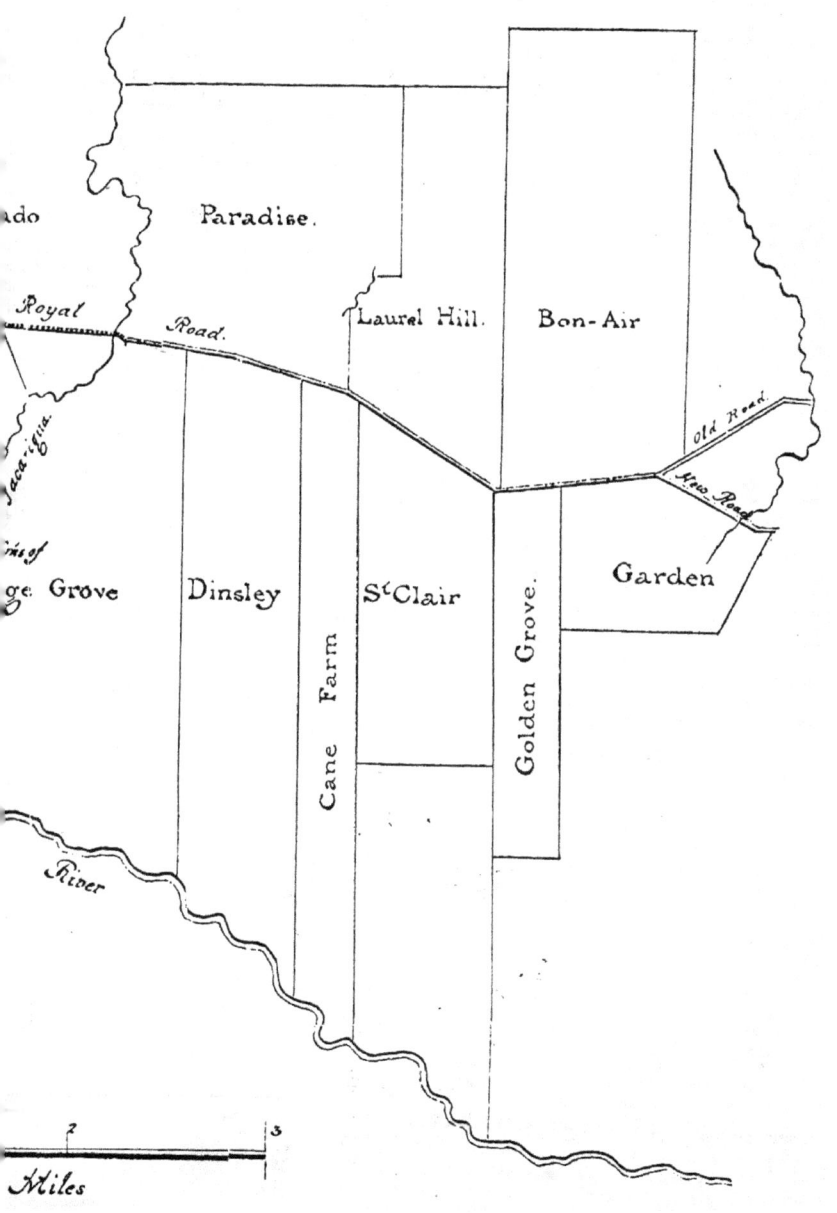

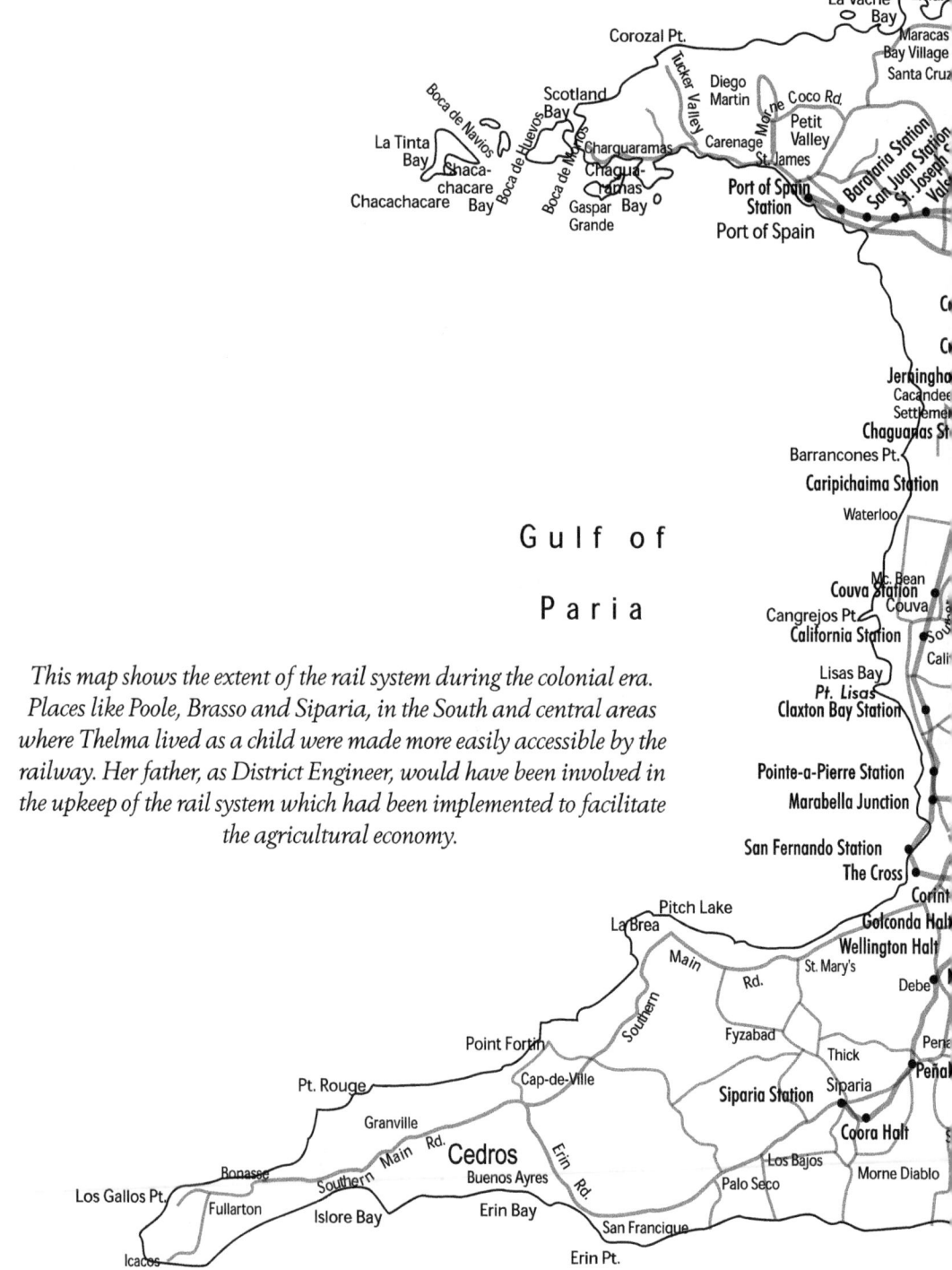

This map shows the extent of the rail system during the colonial era. Places like Poole, Brasso and Siparia, in the South and central areas where Thelma lived as a child were made more easily accessible by the railway. Her father, as District Engineer, would have been involved in the upkeep of the rail system which had been implemented to facilitate the agricultural economy.

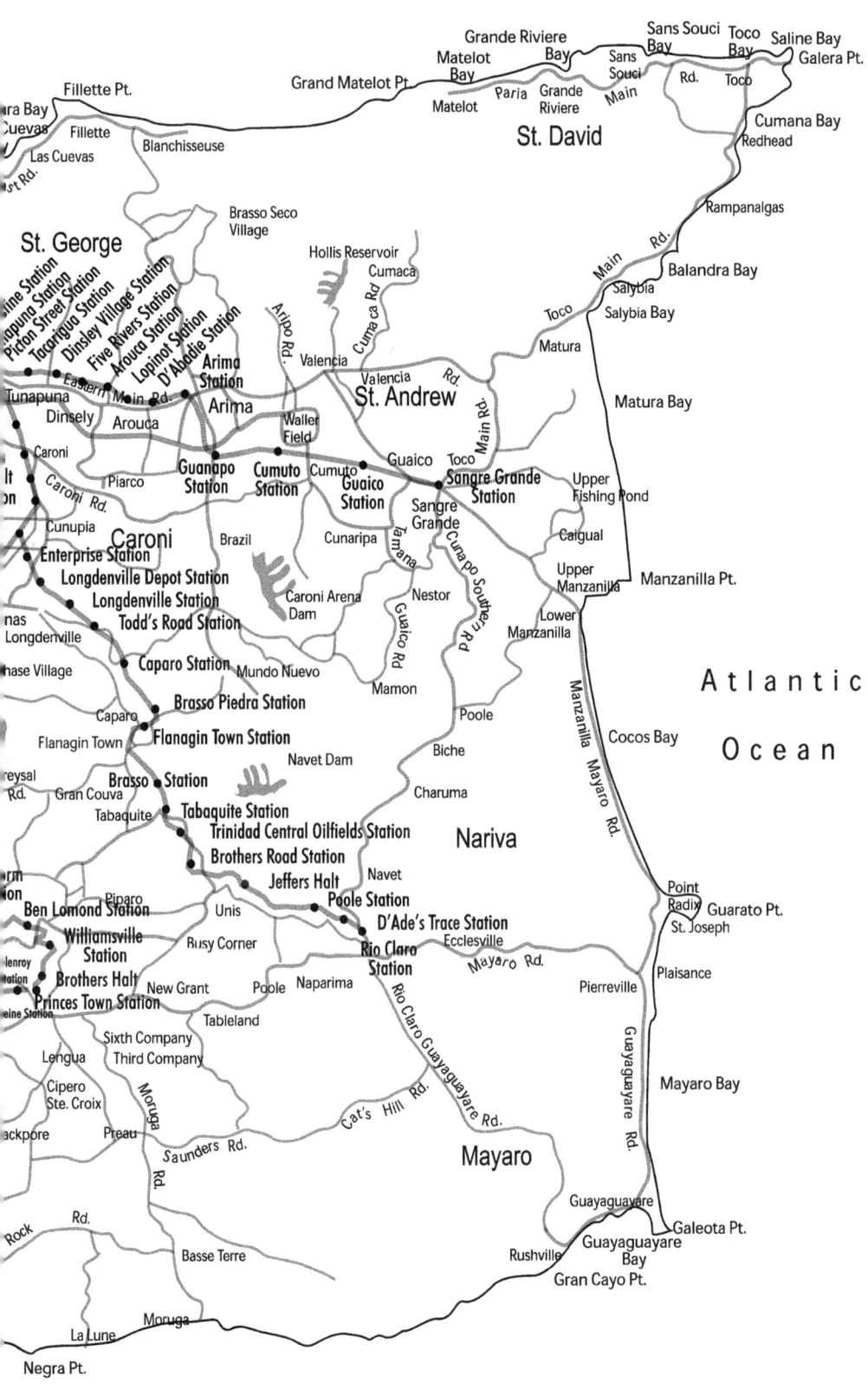

 Poole

*W*HEN I WAS ABOUT 2-1/2 YEARS OLD my father was transferred to Poole, which is in the south of Trinidad, and this is where my first childhood memories start. I dimly remember a low rambling house with many jalousies—in those days all the houses were built with jalousies which could be opened and closed (an old-fashioned version of louvres) and there were usually wide verandahs all around the house which cut off the glare and the direct sun from the living rooms and bedrooms. This always gave these rooms a cool look and the masses of ferns and palms on the verandah added to this feeling. On a blazing hot day outside, it was a great comfort to walk into the shady verandah and cool rooms. Modern architecture with its concrete and glass has lost this calm and cool look and feel. I seem to remember it was always raining, but there are certain incidents that stand out very clearly.

My other godmother, Camilla Siegert, a very rich lady who travelled extensively, had just come back from Germany. The Siegerts were a German family and she had brought back a beautiful doll for me. I was playing with the doll and it fell on the stone floor of the verandah and its beautiful china face broke into pieces. I remember crying to break my heart and my father took me on his lap and said "never mind, mouche," (that was his nickname for me), "I'll mend it". So we went into his little office (he always had his own little office in every house we ever lived in, where he made all his calculations and plans etc.) And he sat for hours—at least it seemed like hours, but children's idea of time is always out of proportion—while he tried to mend the doll's china face. The beautiful doll's face, however, looked dreadful, as if someone had got to work on it with a knife. The scarred face, with its vacant doll's look, stared at me as if it was all my fault and I just couldn't bear to look at it. So I never played with it again and I never knew what happened to it and never asked.

Another incident I remember very well was going to have lunch and rum punches with some friends on a Sunday. I don't remember who they were or anything about the lunch, I just remember our drive home in our horse and buggy, sitting between my parents who were both in a happy mood and my father saying "I wonder how fast old Bacalow can go" and calling out "gee-up, gee-up, Bacalow, gee-up" and all of us laughing, when suddenly Bacalow started to gallop away.

I also remember someone called 'Mundy'. I later discovered his real name was Munderine (a Swiss geologist) often coming to lunch and I remember my mother saying "what, Mundy coming again, he will eat us out of house and home", but she was always nice to him when he came around and always gave him a nice lunch. I think he liked my mother very much and always told her what beautiful hair she had and in his broken English would say, "Mrs. Emmies with her face like a smiling rose". My father would frown and my mother would blush, but I am sure she loved the compliments. I liked Mundy, he always gave me some little toy (aren't children mercenary, they love people who give them things.) Mundy had red hair and very blue eyes and I can still remember a little what he looked like, he certainly wasn't good-looking. I wonder what happened to him; after we left Poole I never remember seeing him again. I expect he went to some other country, geologists always seem to travel from country to country.

 *Brasso*

My father was then transferred to a place called Brasso. This is a place in the centre of Trinidad, in the cocoa-growing area, at that time. My memories of Brasso are also very vague, as I was only 3-1/2 to 4 years of age. But I do remember the house as being a very high two-storey house at the foot of the hill on the main road.

Of course the only things that one ever saw on the road were people walking with bunches of plantain and bananas on their heads, and men riding horses, mules or donkeys. Occasionally, one saw a horse and buggy pass. At the back of our house were quite a lot of fruit trees, all growing on the slopes of the hill. I remember very well picking and eating mangoes, yellow plums, cherries and tangerine oranges, which are always called Portugal oranges in Trinidad.

It seemed to rain a lot, as I remember the yard always being slushy and muddy and my poor mother having to change me many times in a day. There was a barracks where a lot of Indians lived (now I realise they lived under the most awful conditions, but at the time I took it for granted) and their children were always coming into our garden to pick mangoes and any other fruit that were there. They were always dirty, their clothes ragged and their hair tangled and knotted. My mother was very kind to them and gave them bread and allowed them to pick fruit. But she did not like me to play with them. I don't think that this was because she was prejudiced about their colour, but because she always worried that I would pick up some disease from them. She was always washing my hair and looking carefully to see that I had no lice. The black people of African decent were clean people and never seemed to have lice and their clothes were usually clean. But I think it was because the Indian children were so undernourished, and many had malaria and other sicknesses, that they just didn't have the energy to fetch water to bathe and wash their clothes. I must say these conditions have almost vanished in Trinidad and all the Indian children are always clean and well dressed and their hair shining and combed. This is wonderful to see.

My mother and father hated the barracks, and my father often said. "I wish I could put a match to these barracks and burn them to the ground"—but then the poor people would have nowhere to live. The barracks usually belonged to the cocoa plantations. At that time, cocoa was at a very low price and the cocoa planters did not have the money to build decent houses for their labourers. Although I expect lots of them didn't really care about their labourers.

While we were living in Brasso, I remember a terrible thunderstorm with terrific lightening and thunder that shook the house. It was only my mother and I upstairs, as my father was out at work. I think my mother was frightened as she called Carrington from downstairs, where he was busy cleaning brass and silver cutlery and ornaments, and told him to come and stay upstairs until the storm had passed. This episode is very vivid in my memory.

I also remember Stella Collins, my mother's cousin and very dear friend. My mother said Stella was like a sister to her and she could tell her anything. Stella and her mother were staying with us in Brasso. Aunt Marie Collins is a very vague figure, she seemed to have spent most of the time in her bedroom and Stella and mother always seemed worried about her and they told me she was ill. Years later I realised that she drank very heavily and Stella was so worried about her and thought a change would do her good, so brought her to our house.

I don't think the change helped her as she died not long afterwards and I was never told what the cause of her death was.

 Siparia

We only lived in Brasso for a short time. Engineers were never left long in one place and we were always moving to new places and it was not long before my father was transferred to Siparia. When I was young I loved the excitement of moving to new places, although I expect my mother and father didn't like it very much. My mother especially must have always been packing or unpacking. However, I'm sure that both my father and mother were pleased to leave Brasso. I, of course, was too young to be pleased about it, just as long as I was with my parents all was well.

Whenever my parents had to move, they had workmen from the public works to pack all our things. Aunt Anna usually came to spend some time with us before we moved to help mother with the packing, and when we arrived at our new house was also there to help with the unpacking. Carrington was there too and he did all the hard work of unpacking while mother and Aunt Anna put away things.

My childhood memories of Siparia are very vivid and I remember it as being a very happy time when my mind must have been very receptive to various incidents, people and places.

As there are so many memories from that time to dig from, it is difficult to know where to start. So I will begin by describing our house, also my relations, friends and our servants. People had now begun to play a very important part in my life. Prior to this, the only people who were important had been my parents.

To get to our house, which was on a slight rise, one took a driveway from the Siparia main road up to the house. It was made of pitch from the Pitch Lake, which wasn't very far away. This driveway is very vivid in my imagination, as I remember riding my little tricycle down it very fast, pedalling and going full tilt like the wind. The cuts and bruises that I got on my knees and elbows were innumerable and I always had bandages.

The driveway seemed to be such a long one to me at the time, so I was disappointed when I visited the house about 12 years later and found that it was in fact a very modest little driveway, bordered on both sides by coconut trees, abundant with coconuts, and we always had large jugs of coconut water which my mother and father loved and I did too, especially with the soft jelly in the water.

When we got to the top of the rise, the driveway made a circle like the diagram below:

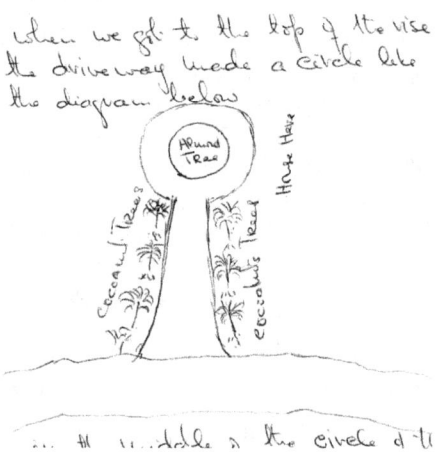

In the middle of the circle was a large almond tree that had branches spread out like a huge umbrella. It was lovely and shady and a place where I played a lot.

Approaching the house was a flight of wide, shallow steps that led into a big verandah. This verandah was where we spent most of our time, as it faced east and was very cool. When the sun rose in the morning, it bathed the verandah with its golden light, and in the afternoon it was cool and shady. It was a long verandah with large Demarara windows, which were made of jalousies and were pushed out with a sturdy stick that fitted into a slotted place in the windowsill.

The windowsills were very wide and mother kept all sorts of potted plants on them, mostly maidenhair ferns that added to the cool feel and look of the verandah.

The verandah ran from north to south. At the north end was a lovely doll's house that my father had had made for me for my fourth birthday. It really was the most beautiful doll's house. A doll's house like that today would cost a fortune. It was very big and the roof nearly reached the ceiling of the verandah, but I will write more about that later. Now I must go on describing the house.

Off the north portion of the verandah, we always called it a gallery, was a door leading into my parents' dressing room, and just off the dressing room was their bedroom. I can't remember details of the bedroom, but I know I slept in a big crib in the bedroom with my parents. At the south end of the verandah was a door leading into another dressing room and another bedroom, which was called the spare room.

There was always someone staying with us, so it was seldom empty. I think there was another bedroom but I don't remember it. In the middle of the house was the living room and then the dining room, with a narrow gallery off of it, a pantry to the southern end, and a bathroom to the northern end. There was a very steep set of wooden steps that led down to the kitchen and the servants' rooms. The front of the house was much nearer the ground than at the back, so I expect it was built on sloping ground.

Thinking now of the back steps leading to the kitchen, it seems to me that there must have been at least twenty, but I expect if the house was still there and I could see it now, it would probably be half that number!

We had two large cisterns—one near the pantry and one near the garage, on which we depended entirely for all the water we used. It rained a lot in Siparia and I don't remember us ever being without water.

A Caledonia wood burning stove of the type that Thelma's parents would have had.

Then there were our servants whom I remember well. There was Carrinngton, who was now a young man. He served at table, dressed in a white tunic and white trousers, passed the vegetables, served the drinks etc. He was also the maker of the drinks for all our guests. In those days everyone drank cocktails and rum punches. Rum was the national drink and only the very wealthy people drank whiskey. Some drank gin. Anyway, Carrington's cocktails became quite famous amongst my parents' friends. A cocktail is made of 1/2 a cocktail glass of rum, 3/4 cocktail glass of crushed ice, a dash of Angostura bitters and a very small amount of sugar or a few drops of cane syrup. These are put into a jug swizzled with a swizzle stick until the mixture gets very frothy, and then it is poured into cocktail glasses. The main thing is, it must be very cold. The measure I have given above is for one cocktail.

Carrington cleaned all the shoes that were put out every morning. He cleaned all the brass and silver, which were always shining so that one could see one's face in them. He cleaned and sharpened the knives every day. He would rub them on a knife board with a sort of powder. I remember very well sitting on the wooden steps at the back of the house with Carrington, helping him clean the shoes. What a nuisance I must have been to him! But he would never let me clean or sharpen the knives. Carrington had been with us since I was born and he was part of my family, someone to whom I could turn if my parents weren't around.

Then there was cook, Modestine. She was a little woman, not black, a light brown with her hair tied up in a brightly coloured handkerchief that was made of heavily starched checkered or striped cotton (sometimes worn with a checkered and striped large handkerchief made of madras muslin, as a shawl with their voluminous skirts. The young girls looked very pretty and attractive with their *tête calendée* set coquettishly on their shiny blue black hair.). My mother liked her a lot and she was a very good cook. She spoke broken English

Indian ajoupa

and preferred to speak in French patois. My father spoke patois well, but my mother couldn't. However, she could always understand Modestine and make herself understood. I can't remember my mother ever going into the kitchen, and am afraid the modern housewife would have been horrified at this. I spent a lot of time with Modestine who would let me help her, and I seem to remember the kitchen being very smokey and dirty. We had a Caledonia stove which burnt wood and it smoked a lot, and Modestine also cooked on coal pots. Anyway, whether the kitchen was dirty or not, the food was always delicious and none of us had any stomach problems.

Modestine was about 50, or maybe it was just that I was so young and all grown up people seemed old! When reading this, one must bear in mind that it is a child's memories and everything is outsize—ages, places and time. One month in a small child's life is like a year of an adult.

Modestine and Carrington both lived in the servants' quarters connected to the main house. Modestine sometimes went home on weekends, but Carrington was always there. Our home was his home.

We also had a gardener, Ackbar, an East Indian who lived in the village close by. He wore the traditional East Indian costume, a capra, which is a cloth tied in such a way as to make a pair of pants, a turban on his head and a jacket. Ackbar lived with his wife and children in a hut made of tapia, called an ajoupa. The walls of these huts are usually made from a mixture of mud, cow dung, dried straw and water, while the roof was made from carat or palm leaves. The framework of the house was made out of wood and outside was plastered with clay. The Indians made their whole house themselves, plastering it with their hands until it was very smooth. Thinking back, ajoupas seemed to me to be one large room divided by coco bags or a coarse sort of cloth hanging from rods, but this I am not sure about, as I don't remember ever going into an Indian's ajoupa house, I just remember looking through the door, and inside always looked dark, as the windows were small. Also, I was scared of all the statues of the different Indian gods that they had in little shrines. The floor of the hut was made of mud (clay) stamped down until it was hard, almost like concrete.

Ackbar and his family lived in the village and we lived just outside the village, but we passed Ackbar's house often and always stopped to speak to his wife and his twin sons. Their yard was always very clean, but very bare, they did not have any plants or flowers. They swept their yard with brooms made of cocoyea and tied securely to bits of straight wood cut from trees and looks like this:

The coconut fiber is where the arrow points and they are made from this:

Cocoyea is the hard fibre in the coconut leaf. The Indians strip the green part off and leave the fibre part, which has many uses like making kites, brooms etc. It is flexible and lasts.

Ackbar's family always seemed to be cleaning brass pots and brass trays. These they shone with limes, cut in half and dipped into ashes and fine sand, until they shone like the sun. They then washed them thoroughly and dried them. They also had brass goblets in which they kept water; we on the other hand kept our water in goblets made of clay that had been baked in ovens (kilns). We had three clay goblets and they were kept on the window sill in the front gallery, and the water in them was always lovely and cool.

Big kettles of water were boiled every day and when the water was cool, my mother filled the clay goblets and we always had clear, cool water for drinking. Those were the days when one depended on large blocks of ice once or twice a week and kept them in big ice boxes packed with sawdust, which helped to make it last longer. We got our ice from San Fernando, but we often ran short, so we were glad of the cool water from the goblets.

I remember Ackbar's asking my mother and father, and of course that included me, to the wedding of his twin sons. They were only twelve years of age and, as far as I can remember, the girls that they were marrying were about nine. Thinking of it now horrifies me, but it was very much the Indian custom in those days and everyone took it for granted, although I know my parents could not have approved. However, they felt that it was the custom of the East Indian and they must be left to solve their own matters. As a matter of fact, I learnt afterwards that after they got married, the girls went back to their parents, and only returned to live with their mothers-in-law when they were about 12, who then trained them in their duties as wives. I expect the little girls were made to work quite hard while the mothers-in-law sat back and gave orders.

I can't remember the wedding, just lots of East Indians sitting down under the trees, and the white people were given chairs. There was a lot of beating of drums and old Indian priests chanting something in Hindi, all of which is vague in my mind.

Besides Carrington, Modestine and Ackbar, we had a maid who swept and dusted, made the beds and polished the furniture, but I don't remember her at all.

It is a funny thing in life that although one remembers the people around you, one can't remember oneself. Looking back I have no idea what I looked like, but from pictures of myself and what I was told, I think I must have been a thin little girl, with very blonde hair (Uncle Harry always called me 'white bat'), freckles, blue-green eyes with specks of brown, and a very fiery temper. The people I loved, I loved so, so much and all animals were precious, even the ones I didn't like, for instance, frogs and lizards. I hated to see anything or anyone hurt. I always wanted to bring all the hurt animals into the house, much to my mother's disgust, and although she was always very kind to them, she was very firm that I keep them in the garage or somewhere outside. The favourite place to hide these wounded or sick creatures was under the house, and I suffered great distress when, after giving them all sorts of things to eat (which was anything I liked to eat, like sweets, sugar cakes or peanuts, no wonder they never got better) they died. My father and mother were always having to console me, and Carrington would say "Miss Thelma, don't cry so much, these things have to die", but I couldn't seem to accept this logic.

It was at this point that my relatives started to play an important part in my life. Aunt Anna, who often stayed with us, made my clothes, dresses to wear in the afternoon and rompers, a sort of bloomer with elastic that held them just above the knees (which made them puff out). I remember I hated the elastic and always found it very uncomfortable and always ended up cutting it. Aunt Anna would get very upset when I did this, as she loved to see me (according to her) like a little picture. Another thing I hated was Aunt Anna combing and brushing my hair and then putting a big ribbon called a butterfly bow in it. I had dozens of these ribbons in every colour, blue checks, red checks and yellow checks. I didn't mind dressing up in the afternoons with my pretty dresses and ribbons, but during the day I hated having to keep clean.

I loved Aunt Anna very much. She was like a second mother to me, and as she never married or had any children, I was the child she never had, the one she loved. I was her goddaughter and she did everything for me, but she also never forgot to scold me if I was in the wrong, or when I got into one of my tantrums and stamped and yelled and behaved abominably. Looking back to those years, I realise that I was a very, very lucky little girl, always surrounded by the people who loved me, but who always told me my faults. But I must add, they always praised me when I was good and told me how sweet I was. I think this is very important to a child, to be praised when good and scolded when at fault, then one knows where one stands.

Soon after we moved to Siparia, my mother got pregnant. I don't remember much about it, except my mother feeling very sick and having to stay in bed. The doctor came to see her, he was a good friend of the family, Dr. Eric de Verteuil, and I remember him very well, as he and his wife and children lived at Pointe-a-Pierre and we often went to see them and they often came to see us. Their

Leo Seheult in Siparia

children were Ulric, who was about a year older than I was, Maureen and Elisa. Dr. de Verteuil told my mother she should have a change and so my mother and I went to spend a month with my grandparents, Aunt Anna, Aunt Muriel, Uncle Jack and Uncle Harry. They all lived together at a house in Gordon Street, in Port of Spain.

My father drove us into Port of Spain. He had just bought a little two-seater Ford car. There was such excitement when he bought this car, it was one of the first Fords, had brass lights and was very high from the ground with brass rods along the side (Carrington took great pride in keeping the brass shining). In those days no one had to get a license to drive, there was no self starter, someone had to crank the car to start it, and this Carrington did when we were at home, but my father had to do it when he was out. Evidently driving a car in those days was very simple compared to these days, mainly because there was no traffic. There were just three pedals, one to start the car and keep it going, one to reverse and one to stop. When we first got it, the whole village ran out to see it, and all the children were waving and calling out to the others to come and see this wonder buggy, going along by itself without a horse. Of course I felt very important sitting beside my father and mother and waving to all the children. After a few months my father got the Public Works carpenter to add a little wooden seat at the back, which could be lifted up, and my father kept all the things he needed for the car in there. This is where I sat with any of my cousins or friends who were staying with us at the time. We were very blown about, but as the car didn't go very fast, we didn't mind. I loved to kneel down in that seat and lean over the back while my father was driving along the country roads, and see all the dry leaves dancing about as the car drove over them. My hair was always in terrible knots afterwards and when I got home, had to have it combed and brushed and this I hated.

The drive from Siparia to Port of Spain was a very long one in those days. The roads were bumpy and twisty and one had to go in a very round about way. It seemed to take ages and ages and I must have gotten very bored and my poor mother must have felt quite car sick. I don't remember much about the drive except that when we got to the old Caroni bridge (which was still there when I was grown up and married), my father stopped and we had a cold drink from a thermos flask and mother said "look at Mount St. Benedict right on top of that Hill". I always remember that and seeing Mount St. Benedict for the first time.

Carrington had come with us in case the car broke down or if we had a puncture, which was a common occurrence in those days. I know that my father slept that night at Gordon Street, and somewhere must have been found for Carrington to sleep. My father left the next day.

I enjoyed staying with my grandparents and old aunts and uncles in Gordon Street. It was quite an experience for a small child from the country to come and stay in Port of Spain. Everything was so fascinating; turning on the electric lights was like magic. I was so accustomed to the oil lamps which had to be put out each morning to have their wicks trimmed and the glass shades washed and shone and oil put into the lamps to be ready for the night—so it really seemed like magic to just turn a switch and a light came on. I also loved the tram cars. Aunt Muriel used to take me, Joy, Ena and Phyllis to the Botanical Gardens every Sunday afternoon to listen to the police band. It was very exciting and we loved going in the tram car which ran around the Savannah. I remember auntie opening her little silver purse, which was just for tram tickets, and paying the man who came around to collect them.

I still remember the tram driver, he had light brown skin and was tall and very erect, and he seemed such an important person doing a very important job. When we got to the gardens, auntie usually met some friends and they sat down and chatted and we children ran around, climbed trees and caught tadpoles from around the fountain. It was all so wonderful and so different from anything I had ever done before.

I also remember all the street cries in the early morning, the women with big trays on their heads calling out—"Get your nice sweet plantains, plantains to fry and boil", the woman selling fish calling out "poisson fraiche, come, come and get your nice fresh fish", and the man selling oysters, a Chinaman dressed all in black with long baggy trousers and jacket with wide sleeves and a very wide straw hat calling out "loysters, loysters". Mother always called him in and he would open the oysters there and add a little pepper sauce from a bottle that he kept with his oysters. Mother loved oysters, I thought they were awful.

The Gray children spent many days at grandma's house and we played all sorts of games, climbed the mango tree and pretended it was a ship, and most of all we used to love to go to the Chinese shops just next door to grandma's and buy hot penny hops bread and go home where Aunt Anna would cut them in half and put a dab of butter, which immediately melted. It was delicious. In the evenings after dinner, which was usually a hot cup of cocoa with condensed milk, Johnny cakes (bakes) and scrambled egg, we all played card games, or grandma would play the piano and we would all dance about.

Auntie would take us with her to see "Old Emily", who was an old Portuguese woman who lived with her daughter in Belmont. We would go about once a week and auntie, who belonged to the "Les Aimantes de Jesus", used to collect money and clothes, sheets, towels etc. from her friends and these we took for them. Old Emily was always so glad to see us, and though she was very poor, her room was always clean and tidy and so was she. I don't remember anything more about her as I went back to Siparia and I forgot about her, but I'm sure auntie, Aunt Anna & grandma continued to look after her. Then they were all the different servants that were there, I remember Juanita and her daughter Muinets, she was the washer and came every Monday to collect all the dirty clothes and to bring back the clean ones.

The clean clothes were a sight to behold as all the frills on the blouses and all the lace around the wrist and neck were so beautifully ironed and all standing out. Juanita was very proud of her washing and ironing and she loved grandma

The house of the Miss Dragos on Marine Square in the background.

dearly, she always called her "Mama". Eventually Juanita went to New York where she made a lot of money washing and ironing for the rich Americans. She used to write to grandma and send her presents as she said she was doing so well. Poor Juanita, she saved up enough money to come back to Trinidad and buy herself a nice house for her old age, but she fell into the hands of an unscrupulous lawyer who robbed her of nearly everything. Grandma was terribly upset about it, but there was nothing she could do except sympathise with poor Juanita and make her welcome when she came to see her. Then there was "Perseverance", a shoemaker who came to Gordon Street every morning to ask if there were any shoes to be repaired, there usually weren't but grandma said he certainly had perseverance, and that was the only name we ever knew him by.

There were so many things to do in Port of Spain, I remember going to see the two Miss Dragos with Aunt Anna. They lived right downtown in Port of Spain near to the Roman Catholic cathedral. That used to be the fashionable part of Trinidad when they were young women, but by then it had become very slummy. I remember so well this wooden door in a great big wall, and Aunt Anna ringing a big bell and the door being opened by someone, I have no recollection who, and then it was like going into another world. There was a lovely fountain and

The Hall, where Camilla Siegert, my godmother, lived.

lots of maidenhair ferns and other kinds of ferns and a long flight of stone stairs leading up into the house. I loved the two Miss Dragos, Josephine and Eugenie, they always made such a fuss over me, and I would recite for them and dance for them and they said I was wonderful, and of course I felt wonderful. They always had delicious biscuits and sweets and I was always given some to take home. They spoke mainly in French, but to me they spoke in English. I can still hear them saying "here comes dear Anna with 'le petit elève'".

When I grew up and got married to Archie and we had our first baby, Ian, the Miss Dragos gave me a most beautiful mahogany carved crib. There wasn't a nail in it and it could all be completely unscrewed and put away. I hate to relate that I was a most awful vandal and thought the crib too dark for a baby and painted it white! I was young and foolish.

The two Miss Dragos were very attached to each other and when Eugenie died, Josephine died a few days after. They were old and just couldn't live one without the other. I often wonder what happened to all their beautiful antique furniture, everything they had in the house was an antique and in these modern times would have been worth a fortune.

At another occasion, grandma and Aunt Anna took me to visit Aunt Camilla Siegert (as I mentioned before, she was my godmother). The house she lived in was a vast place, at least it seemed vast to a five year old. It was called "the Hall" and is now Bishop Anstey's Girls High School.

When we arrived, Aunt Camilla was sitting in the drawing room and she was glad to see grandma and Aunt Anna. I think she didn't like children very much and she put out her cheek for me to kiss. I didn't like Aunt Camilla, like I loved the Miss Dragos. She called the butler, who was white, and told him to take me around the house. I can't remember much about the house except that all the rooms looked huge. But I remember the pantry very well. It was a long room with a long table and the table was covered with silver cutlery for the table, candle sticks and lots of other things, and there were two maids busily cleaning it all. Then there was the gentleman's room, where there were all sorts of games for them to play; a billiard table, bridge tables and another big table with small mechanical horses and jockeys, which was worked by mechanical means and evidently the men placed bets on the different horses. It was a room to gamble in, although I only knew this later on in my life. The butler then took me into the garden, which was very formal with paths and fountains and beautiful beds of roses and other flowers. After we had seen all this, the butler took me back to the drawing room and I told Aunt Camilla good-bye and much to my relief, we left for Gordon Street.

It wasn't long after this visit that the Siegerts lost a lot of their money. It was on account of World War 1 and that the Siegerts were Germans. Aunt Camilla was so shocked when they told her that she was no longer as rich as she was that she lost her memory, and from then on went into decline. The Siegerts, however, never gave up the secret of Angostura bitters and after a few years had passed, they were as wealthy as they had ever been, although they never lived in the affluence that they were previously used to. Those days were past as after the war, nothing was ever quite the same again.

Uncle Jack played a big part in my life while I stayed at Gordon Street in Port of Spain. I remember him so well riding his bicycle all dressed up in a dark grey suit with a very stiff collar and a tie. I don't know where he went to, but he always came back with something for us children (the Grays and I); usually it was a great big bunch of yellow Portugal oranges which were as sweet as sugar and which we all loved.

Uncle Jack had a lovely dog called "Shackleton". He was a very big black and white dog and Uncle Jack was devoted to him and he to Uncle Jack. He was also very good with us children and we played all sorts of games with him in the yard and under the house. Shackleton was not allowed in the house, as grandma didn't like dogs in the house, but he seemed quite contented to stay outside and had a nice big kennel in the stable where he slept at night. Grandma didn't have a horse and buggy, so the stable was empty.

There was a tragedy about Shackleton: Uncle Jack put down poison for the rats and Shackleton ate some and died. Uncle Jack was completely bereft as he was a very kind man who loved children and animals and Shackleton especially, and the thought that he had been the cause of Shackleton's death was terrible for him. I was living in Tobago when this happened and I can remember how sad I was when mother got a letter from auntie telling her about Shackleton and she telling me about it.

I haven't mentioned much about grandpa Gray, but he was an old man and was very quiet and spent most of his time reading and painting. He painted many pictures, mostly of country scenes and rivers with bamboo trees and native women washing clothes at the riverside. I often wondered what happened to all the pictures he painted. Mother had some in our house in Tobago but after that I never saw them again, and of course children don't think of these things much. Grandpa used to come out for meals but most of the time he spent reading and painting in his room. I sometimes went into his room to see him and he was always glad to see me and always gave me an extra strong peppermint out of a glass jar. I don't remember much more about him as he died when I was still very young.

Well, the month in Port of Spain was now ended, mother was feeling a lot better and daddy was missing us a great deal. Mother and I were sad at leaving grandma, grandpa and the aunts and uncles, but glad to be going home to see daddy and all my toys and doll's house waiting for us. A child is always excited at any move and although I would miss Ena, Joy and Phyllis (the Grays) I was excited at seeing at seeing daddy, Carrington and Modestine.

I knew that the Grays would come to stay with me and Aunt Anna had promised to come soon to help mother with all the baby clothes and things for the crib, nets, etc. Daddy and Carrington came to meet us and once more we were back in Siparia.

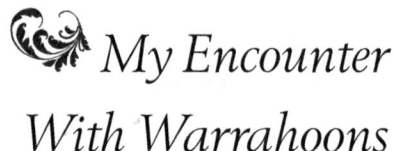 My Encounter With Warrahoons

THERE ARE SO MANY MEMORIES OF SIPARIA that it is hard to tell them all. One particular memory is of the Warrahoons, a tribe of Amerindians (indigenous natives) who came over from the wilds of Venezuela in small dug out canoes. They used to land at Palo Seco Beach and then run inland. They could not speak any tongue that anyone knew, and they seemed to me to grunt and growl a lot. They wore no clothes and always had lots of monkeys, parrots and some hammocks which they made out of some sort of twine.

Money meant nothing to them, and they only wanted things like brightly coloured bead necklaces and any clothes that you gave them. Mother always kept a trunk full of things for the Warrahoons, so that when they came, she always had something to give them. I was terrified of them and when I heard Carrington and Modestine call out "Madame, lock up the house, the Warrahoons are coming", I used to dash inside and get under the bed. However, my curiosity always got the better of me and when I heard them in the gallery jabbering away and putting on all the clothes and necklaces that mother gave them, I came out and looked at them through a slit in the door. They were always amazed to see themselves in the mirror that mother had hanging in the gallery and which reflected a picture of the big almond tree in it. They would shout and grab at the image in the mirror. When they had dressed up and mother had given them some water to drink, they left yelling and screeching down the driveway. It was really a very incongruous sight.

I was always relieved to see them go. However, I think they must have been very peaceful people as I never heard of them attacking anyone and mother was never afraid of them. Many years later I asked someone from that area what happened to the Warrahoons and did they still come into Palo Seco beach? They told me that the government had stopped them coming as it was thought they brought diseases with them such as small pox and alastrim (a milder form of small pox). Poor things, I wonder what happened to them when they were turned back? I hope they were given water and provisions to get them back home. I expect many of them were drowned on the journey from Venezuela to Trinidad, if they got caught in bad weather in those small dug out canoes.

Warrahoons from down the main

It was now 1916. World War I was raging in Europe and of course affecting the whole world. Daddy's two brothers, Uncle Robert and Uncle André, had both gone, and Uncle Bertie Harragin (*note 4*) had joined the West India Regiment and was fighting in Egypt and Palestine. Uncle Bertie was my mother's first cousin and as his father had died before he was born, he was brought up with mother and her brothers Willie and Gus and older sister Muriel, so he was very close to them. Victor Collins and another cousin, Leonard Sorzano, were all away fighting in France.

Naturally the war was a great topic of conversation amongst the grown-ups as most people had someone of theirs fighting in this terrible war. As a child I heard the grown-ups speaking about all the terrible atrocities the Germans had committed, especially in Belgium. I thought of the Germans as some sort of terrible monsters and I was very afraid that they would come to Trinidad and kill all the people I loved. I used to have nightmares about them, and when the Indians began to beat their drums at night, I was sure it was the Germans coming from Palo Seco beach, so I used to take my pillow and crawl into bed with mother and daddy and then I was consoled and felt safe.

One day daddy came home and said to my mother, "Emmie, Mr. Baird (he was an American supervisor at the oilfields in Palo Seco) has said that there is an oil well that they expect to gush this afternoon and would we like to go to his house and see it." Mother said yes, she would, and of course they brought me too. Mr. Baird's house was on a hill and we had a good view of the oilfields, and the well did come in with a terrific force and then they had to try and stop the oil flowing. It must have been a very exciting moment when the well gushed, but I was too young to really appreciate it.

It was when we lived in Siparia that I got my first book. Daddy bought me a beautiful book of "Alice in Wonderland". I am sure it was a first edition; it had so many lovely pictures of Alice going down the rabbit hole, the white rabbit taking his watch out of his pink waistcoat pocket, Alice sitting with the Mad Hatter and the door mouse at the Mad Hatter's tea party, and so many others that it would take too long to mention them all. My father read me the whole book, he sitting in his favourite chair on the gallery and I sitting on his lap. I will never forget this and I will never forget the book; it has always been my favourite child's story, and I am sure it was because daddy read it with such expression, and I could look at all the beautiful, coloured pictures and visualise the whole thing. This was my introduction to books and I have loved them ever since. Books were always my favourite presents.

Then came the excitement of the baby's birth. I think mother must have sent me to spend the day with some friends, probably I went to Robert and Caro de Verteuil's house, they were good friends of my parents and I liked Louis, their son, who was the same age as I was, and I loved the big yard with all the animals, horses and donkeys, ducks and fowls. It was big cocoa estate which Robert looked after, and I and all the other children used to play outside all day and also in the cocoa fields which were always shady and cool with large immortelle trees shading the cocoa. The cocoa tree has to have shade and the immortelle tree was always called "The Mother of the Cocoa".

In the afternoon I went home and daddy said "come and see your baby sister" and there lying in the crib was a baby. I really don't remember what she looked like, but I know I loved her very much. I wanted to lift her up right away but my mother said "she is still too small, but you will soon be able to lift her up". For a few days I spent lots of time with the baby, but then other things began to interest me and although I loved my baby sister, I continued with all the things that interested me.

One day daddy came home and said "I think we should all go to see the Pitch Lake". The Pitch Lake was near La Brea and so we set off. I imagined the Pitch

Lake to be a big sort of pool full of oil, like I had seen gushing out of the well at Palo Seco, so I was very disappointed when I saw it was like a very big pond with pitch just like we saw on the roads. Daddy said "let's walk over it, it is quite firm". I was a little nervous at first at the thought of walking on it, but when mother and daddy began to walk I soon followed them. It was soft walking on it and our shoes made an imprint on the surface, with some places softer than others. There were also pools of water on it from the rain that had fallen the night before. It seemed to me to be quite a long way to walk. When we got to the other side, my father said "now remember this, Thelma, it is one of the wonders of the modern world, for no matter how much pitch they take out, it is always as full as it was before". I don't know if this is true today, for they must have taken out vast amounts over the years, but then it certainly didn't look as if any pitch had been taken out. Even though at the time I found it boring, I am glad my father brought me to see the Pitch Lake, as I don't remember ever going there again. I think my mother was a bit disappointed as well.

After going to the Pitch Lake, daddy said "Let's go to see Eric de Verteuil", who was a friend of my parents and also a doctor and attended to us when we were sick. Dr. de Verteuil, his wife Netta and their children lived in a new bungalow which the Americans had built for the them and all their other staff. I thought it was an awful house all enclosed with mosquito netting, and I felt I was in a cage. I said "I don't like this house very much," and Dr. de Verteuil said "if you lived in a house like this you wouldn't get that bad malaria that you get". I expect he was right and that is why the Americans had insisted that their staff all lived in houses like cages so that the mosquitoes couldn't get in and bite them and give them malaria. When I used to get attacks of malaria, I felt terrible, burning hot with fever, yet shivering so much that the whole bed seemed to shake. I couldn't swallow the quinine capsule, so my mother had to give me quinine powder mixed in jam or condensed milk to try to disguise the taste. It was so bitter that no matter how much jam mother put in to try and mask the bitterness, I could always taste that terrible bitter taste. Mother usually mixed it with raspberry jam, and up to now, in my old age, I can still taste that bitter taste if I eat raspberry jam, so of course I never eat it. I used to get a bout of malaria every few months and I know that my parents worried a lot about me. Monica, my baby sister, never seemed to get it. I think I must have got it when we lived at Poole or Brasso, which were such wet places and full of mosquitoes and the people around must have had it. My mother and father also never got malaria!

Muriel Evans getting off a tramcar in Port of Spain, 1920's

84 Dundonald Street in 1995, where Emily Seheult née Gray lived with her sister Muriel Evans née Gray and great great Aunt Anna Collins from 1939 until her death in 1956.
(Standing in front of the house are Bonnie Northrup née Huggins, Michael Huggins, Sandy McKay née Huggins, Roger Huggins and Ken Huggins, children of Monica Huggins née Seheult, Thelma's younger sister)

Muriel Evans

 # Tobago

My father then got transferred to Tobago, and my mother was very distressed at the idea of leaving Trinidad and all her beloved relations, especially her mother and father. Also, Tobago had a very bad reputation for men taking to drinking too much, and as my father was very fond of his cocktails and rum punches, my mother worried that he would drink too much.

Aunt Anna came down to Siparia by train to help mother with the packing and to make some clothes for Monica and me. It was lovely having her with us and she was a great help to mother. I forgot to say that while we lived in Siparia, mother, Monica and I used to go by train to Port of Spain sometimes, to spend a few days with grandma and the others.

It was always a great adventure and when mother said "we are going to spend a few days with grandma and we are going by train" I got very excited. I loved going in the train and going through the tunnel where it got as dark as night in the train and then we would suddenly come out of the tunnel into bright sunshine. When we arrived in Port of Spain there was such hustle and bustle and boys calling out "get your paper, read the latest telegram about the war". The war was still raging and everyone was very worried. Victor Collins had been killed in France and Leonard Sorzano, Violet's husband, had died of typhoid while in hospital in France, so the families were all very sad.

I remember the time mother got a telegram from grandma saying that Audrey Collins had died of the Spanish flu (the Spanish flu was a terrible flu that killed

Steaming by train to Siparia

hundreds of thousands of people all over the world, it was called the Spanish flu because it started in Spain) and that Stella, her sister, had it as well. Mother was in a terrible state as Audrey and Stella Collins were like her sisters, Stella especially. Mother told daddy she would have to go to Port of Spain to be with the family. Daddy's car had broken down, so he couldn't bring us and we went by train. When we got to Port of Spain, mother took a cab—that is a horse-drawn cab—and told the cabbie to drive her to Mrs. Gray's house in Gordon Street. He knew the family and where they lived and so we were soon there. It was very sad, everyone was crying and the house seemed full of people who had come in to sympathise, for since mother had got the telegram in Siparia, Stella had died. The Spanish flu was very contagious, and the doctor said no one was to go to the house, and this was very sad for the family who wanted to be there and to help out in any way they could. I don't remember this visit very well, except that everyone was sad and lots of people were coming and going.

Amongst those I remember coming was Aunt Camilla Siegert and her adopted daughter Viola. They came in a big carriage and I know that grandma was glad to see Aunt Camilla, who she was very fond of. Aunt Camilla had no children, so she adopted Viola de Craney, a niece of hers. Viola inherited all the money Aunt Camilla had after she died. She got married and went to live in Canada, and the story was that Viola's husband spent all the money and left Viola penniless and she died in absolute poverty. I thought of poor Aunt Camilla who thought that she had left Viola well off and with everything she wanted in life.

Mother and I spent about a week at Gordon Street and I really remember very little of what I did. I was told that I had to be very good and quiet as everyone was feeling sad. So I was glad to get back home and go on with my life, though I expect my mother didn't get over her grief for a long time.

Then we were ready to leave for Tobago, everything was packed and sent into Port of Spain and mother, daddy, Monica, I and Carrington all went to spend a few days with the family at Gordon Street. However, when time came to leave, very serious riots broke out in Port of Spain, and daddy told us that they couldn't send our furniture and belongings by ship as the rioters were throwing everything into the sea. We were only allowed to bring our clothes and they said they would send the other things later on. Daddy was then told we would have to stay at Government House in Tobago until our belongings could be sent over safely.

There were quite a lot of us going to Tobago; mother, daddy, Monica, I, Carrington, a nurse mother got in Port of Spain to be with us in Tobago, and Ivy Hughes. How mother decided to bring Ivy with us to Tobago will always be a mystery to me. Aunt Anna was supposed to come to help mother settle in, but my grandfather had taken quite ill and my grandmother wanted Aunt Anna to stay and help her, so much to mother's disappointment Aunt Anna couldn't come. But who suggested Ivy I really can't imagine. She was a complete liability from the time we set foot on the ship for Tobago.

We set sail for Tobago on the *Belize*. It was a Royal Mail Steamer and all the carpets in the cabin, the towels, sheets etc. were all marked in big letters "R.M.S.P (Royal Mail Steam Packet). I was very excited to be on a ship and to be going across the sea; but poor mother was very sea-sick and couldn't even go down for dinner. Mother, daddy, Monica and I were in one big cabin and they had put a crib in for Monica. Ivy and Mary (the nurse who mother had hired to look after Monica and I) shared a cabin and Ivy said she was too ill to move, so Mary must get her something to eat. My father was very annoyed over the whole affair. I don't know where Carrington slept.

Early the next morning, daddy woke me up and said "look out of the port-hole and you will see Tobago", so I looked out and I can still remember how disappointed I was that there was no snow. I had thought that once I went in a ship overseas, the place I was going to was sure to have snow.

I told daddy "But daddy, there is no snow". My father tried to explain that we were still in the West Indies and there wouldn't be any snow. I don't think I really understood but I accepted it.

Poor mother was feeling very sea-sick and sent daddy to call Mary to come and dress Monica and I, but Mary was looking after Ivy and couldn't come. That was what Ivy was like, she never helped and she always had to be looked after.

The next thing I remember was getting into a small rowing boat and being brought into Scarborough harbour. Daddy was worrying about his car (which he had managed to bring along with us) that they would let it fall into the sea when they were putting it on the barge. However, it arrived safely and we all went to Government House. I don't quite know how Carrington and Mary got there, but they arrived too.

Government House in Tobago was a lovely house. It was a one storey building. The bedrooms were big and all had French windows leading out to a gravelled path and to a garden of lawns and flowering shrubs. The grounds of Government House were big and there were all kinds of fruit trees, mangoes, chenette, plums, sugar apple and lots of others.

The other rooms in Government House were also large, without much furniture in the rooms and with high ceilings. All around the walls of the dining room were busts of the former governors of Tobago. I was too young at the time to notice the names of the governors, but later on in life, when I married Archie, I found out that family legend has it that his great-grandfather known as Baynes. The Baynes she was referring to was Edwin Donald George Vincent Baynes, 1828-1884, Colonial Secretary of the Leeward Islands and 'sometime' Governor of Tobago. He was Archie's mother's grandfather, and his bust was one of those in the dining room. (When we were visiting Tobago and staying at Friendship Estate, Archie and I went to see if we could see the bust of his great-grandfather, but Government House was closed to visitors, so our visit was in vain. However, we did find out that after Trinidad and Tobago became independent, all the busts of former governors had been removed. They didn't realise that they were destroying history).

To go back to our stay at Government House. I loved staying there, the house was so big and there were so many things for a small child to do and discover. Carrington used to help me explore. Monica was too young and daddy and

Government House in Tobago, photographed in the 1890s. It would not have changed much by the time we lived there.

mother were occupied with their own things to do. There was a housekeeper at Government House, her name was Mrs. Hughston who lived in an apartment on the grounds. I often used to go to see Mrs. Hughston and she gave me sugar cakes made out of grated coconuts. She used to make them herself and they tasted very nice.

The day after we arrived in Tobago, daddy said he needed a few things, so mother, daddy and I went into Scarborough (we left Monica with Mary and Ivy). When we arrived in Scarborough there were crowds and crowds of people shouting and yelling, and they had sticks and stones in their hands. My father realised that there was a riot and tried to turn around and go back to Government House, but the people crowded round the car and we couldn't move. Daddy spoke very quietly to them and said he couldn't do anything about their problems as we had only just arrived in Tobago, but when he got to his office the next day, he would hear their complaints. I was very frightened and so was my mother. I expect my father was afraid too, but he didn't let people see this. Anyway, they dispersed and left the car and daddy turned back and we returned to Government House. Since that occasion, with the memory of all those angry people crowded around the car and us feeling so helpless, I have always been afraid of mobs. The road to Government House was deserted and

HMS Hood

we got back safely, but I suppose my parents were very apprehensive about what may happen next.

Government House had a long open gallery in the front and when we sat there we could see the sea. That afternoon all of us were sitting in the gallery when suddenly my father said "look, there is a big battleship coming into Tobago". It was HMS *Hood*. Everyone gave a sigh of relief as we knew that now, with the British sailors here to protect us, we would be safe. None of us realised what a serious riot it had been, with the warden leaving the Court House and riding a horse up to the fort to send a message to Trinidad (I think) for help. He had just managed to get the message off when a whole crowd of rioters came up and burnt down the telegraph office. The warden had got away safely.

However, in Scarborough, where the crowd were getting very out of hand, the riot act had been read and the police had started shooting. As is always the case, three innocent people were shot, one was a shoemaker who was going home and had nothing to do with the riot, and I didn't know who the others were. About two or three hours after, we saw the battleship and we got a message that four sailors were going to be sent to Government House to protect people and property. Mother was a bit put out at the idea of having four young men to feed, but daddy said "don't worry, I expect it will only be for a few days."

So mother went to tell Mrs. Hughston to prepare two bedrooms for the sailors. I am not sure if they were sailors or petty officers, anyway, I thought of them as sailors. They arrived and were very nice and helpful, two were on duty while two were off. The ones on duty had to stand at either end of the bow-shaped driveway leading in and out of Government House. They had to stand with their rifles and bayonets fixed and challenge anyone who wanted to come into Government House or anyone passing who looked suspicious. I think they must have been very bored, as few people came to Government House and very few people even passed on the road as it was in the country part of Tobago.

Police marching band, Tobago 1918

The sailors who were off duty played a lot with me. They taught me how to play marbles, made kites for me and then taught me how to fly them. They helped me climb the fruit trees and pick fruit. I really enjoyed having the sailors at Government House, as Monica was still too young to romp about with me and I had no young children to play with.

In due course, our furniture and belongings arrived, and we then moved to our house up on the Fort Hill. It was a lovely, big, roomy house in a fabulous spot, and we all liked it. There were five bedrooms, one of which mother made into a playroom for Monica and me, where we kept our toys and could play all our games. There was a front gallery, not very big, with a long flight of steps leading up to it. There was a drawing room, a dining room and a long stone gallery at the back which was on a level with the lawn. This gallery was enclosed with trellis work and daddy's office was at one end and the bathroom and lavatory were at the other. It was in this gallery and lawn, which faced east, that mother, daddy and all their friends used to sit in the afternoons. There was a big cistern in the yard and my friends and I spent a lot of time on top of this cistern and made up all kinds of games. It was a long cistern with a rounded top, where we got all our water. There was a hand pump and Carrington used to pump the water up to an overhead tank that supplied the house. I forgot to mention that the day after we went to live at the Fort, HMS *Hood* was still in Tobago as they didn't know if any trouble would start up again, and there was a sentry just outside our back gate. That night mother gave the cook money to go to market to buy some meat, vegetables and fruit to bring home the next day. When the cook got outside the gate, the sentry called out "who goes by, friend or foe?" The cook just took one look at the gun by his side and came in shouting "Lawd, Lawd, he nearly done shoot me!"

Daddy went out to see what all the commotion was about and saw the sailor looking very surprised. He said "I only asked her who goes by, friend or foe, and she started to yell and scream". I think she was naturally terrified and couldn't understand what she was supposed to do and she refused to go home and slept in the servants' quarters.

It was in Tobago that I began to have a lot of friends. There were the Meadins, who lived next door and they had three children, Cicily, Henry and Pamela. Cicily was older than I was, but Henry and Pamela were about my age. Then there were the Purvis children a little way down the hill, they had two girls, Margaret and Betty. I liked Betty, Margaret was very pretty but stuck-up and none of us liked her very much. Their father was a sea captain and was away most of the time, and their mother had a very bad reputation. Of course this I learned from overhearing the grown-ups speaking.

Then there were the Sorzanos, who lived opposite to us, and these were my really good friends. Edris, Stella and Zena were a good bit older than I was but Norma and Ianthe Guppy (she lived with the Sorzanos as her mother was very ill and was in a home) were just about my age and we got on very well together. I liked Mrs. Sorzano very much. Mother liked her too. She had known her in Trinidad. She was called "Fly"—it was a nickname, but I never heard or knew her real name. Mr. Sorzano was a rather silent man and I was a little bit afraid of him. He didn't have a car and rode a horse called "Sugar". Thinking of it now, I wonder how the Sorzanos ever went anywhere, not having a car or a buggy.

The Sorzanos had a governess for the girls. She was a young girl called Gertrude Watson and she taught them and stayed with them if Mr. and Mrs. Sorzano went out, although I don't seem to remember them going out. It seemed to me that Gertrude Watson lived all the time with the Sorzanos.

Mother asked Mrs. Sorzano if I could go to school with Miss Watson as I was now old enough to be going to school (of course mother paid Miss Watson). So it was arranged that I should go to school with the Sorzanos. It was very convenient as the house was just opposite and I could go over by myself. I was doing the same sort of work as Norma and Ianthe and I liked Miss Watson very much. She came from another island in the Caribbean, an island called Antigua. (It was in Antigua that I spent the later years of my life with my husband who came from Antigua).

I seemed to spend a lot of my time at the Sorzanos, they had a huge house and Mr. Sorzano was the magistrate and this was the house the magistrates lived in. There was a gallery around the whole top of the house, all enclosed, and this was where we had school and where we played and had all our dolls and toys. Mrs. Sorzano never seemed to mind what confusion we made as long as we didn't make a disorder in the bedrooms and drawing room, or bother her while she was in the pantry making some of her delicious cakes and pastries.

Under the Sorzano house were prison cells and each door had a number on it. In the former days this was the jail and I don't know who lived upstairs in those days, perhaps it was a prison warden or perhaps it was always the magistrate that lived there. I know as a little girl, I never liked going downstairs and seeing the cells with their numbers as I imagined the prisoners being locked up in these cells, and I very seldom went down there.

It was around this time that I began to have pets. Daddy bought me a baby goat, it was pure white and it was the cutest little thing and daddy got a little collar for it. However, it did not make a good pet as it was always running away and I expect it didn't like being fussed over. I soon got tired of it and Carrington used to take it out to the pasture in front of the house and leave it there to graze. Daddy realised that it really wasn't a suitable pet and gave it away to one of the overseers at the Public Works Department.

Then, a few months after, daddy and mother went to see the de Nobrigas at Lowlands Estate. They had a lot of sheep and there was a lovely little lamb which they let me hold. Mr. de Nobriga said "would you like that little lamb?" Naturally I was thrilled at having this lovely little lamb, but my mother was hesitant, especially when Mr. de Nobriga said I would have to give it milk out of a baby's bottle four times a day. Anyway, we took the lamb home and mother found a baby's bottle (probably one of Monica's when she was a baby) and I fed it and it drank well. For a day or two I did this, but then I began to get bored and Carrington took over the task of feeding it. It grew up but I don't think it was very healthy, and one day it looked very ill and daddy got the vet who said he didn't think it would live. I didn't know what was the matter with it, anyway it died and as it was the first thing that I had ever seen dead. I was very, very upset and very glad when they took it away.

After this my mother said "no more pets". And I was quite satisfied not to have anything more to be worried about.

We hadn't been in Tobago very long when Mary, the nurse who mother had brought from Trinidad, said she was feeling homesick and wanted to go back home, so she was sent back to Trinidad and mother got a very good young woman from Tobago called Frances Baird. We all loved Frances and she was a great help to mother with Monica and I, and also she kept everything clean and tidy and made the most delicious home-made bread. The smell of hot bread pervaded the house and I remember eating hot bread and butter until I could eat no more. Frances stayed with us until I was grown up and got married, and then mother and Frances had a big disagreement and Frances left. We all missed her very much and I'm sorry to say that I never found out where she went to and never went to see her. In a way I thought that if I did I would have been disloyal to mother. But thinking it over mother need never have known. I was wrong, but I was young and just married and full of my own affairs, but none of these things excuse me for not trying to find Frances and going to see her.

Mother also hired a cook called Annie, she really was a gem and she had a wonderful disposition and was never rude and disagreeable. All of us loved Annie. She was in her late forties, I should imagine, and had light brown skin. She wore her hair in two long plaits which she put up behind her head and tied them with a coloured cloth. Annie was with us the whole time we lived in Tobago. And I remember when we were leaving Tobago and Frances was coming with us, mother wanted Annie to come as well, but she said she couldn't leave her children. After we left she went to work for Dr. Krogh and as far as I know stayed with him until she died.

So that was the set up in our house in Tobago. Carrington who served at table, cleaned all the silver and brass and polished the shoes until they shone and did all the other odd jobs. Frances who looked after Monica and I, played cards with us, read us stories (she could read and write very well) did out the rooms and helped mother with lots of other jobs, and Annie who went to market and cooked us delicious meals. She made the most delicious crab backs which we often had.

Our house had two stables, a garage, and a store room away from the house. My father kept his car in the garage and a tank of gasoline in the storeroom well locked up. We children sometimes played in the stables and one day I found a piece of lead, it was long and narrow and very heavy. I don't know for what purpose it was used (*note 5*), but I decided that I would dress it up as a doll and play with it. This was very foolish of me as I had many dolls that I very seldom played with, but children always want something different. I got one of daddy's handkerchiefs which I pinned around it as a skirt and a handkerchief of mother's that I used as a shawl. While I was playing with it, it fell from my hand on the big toe of my right foot. It hurt very much and when I saw all the blood I began shouting to Annie in the kitchen, which wasn't far away. Annie came running and when she saw my toe, she said "Oh my Lawd" and picked me up and wrapped her apron around my toe and ran inside the house with me in her arms to my mother.

When my mother saw the toe she got into a real panic. She rang Dr. Krogh and asked him to come at once. In those days the doctor always came as soon as he could. Dr. Krogh said it was a bad injury. He washed it well with something that burned a lot and when I saw the toe, the nail was off and it looked terrible, and I started to cry again. The doctor bandaged my whole foot and told me I must lie down as he wanted me to keep my foot up and I was not to walk on it until he had seen it again. The toe hurt a lot and mother sat near to me on the bed and read to me and played cards with me. When my father came home, he and Carrington carried me wherever I wanted to go. I felt very important, but the toe still hurt. After a few days Dr. Krogh came back and told me the toe was looking better and told me I could hop around a bit, which I did. He also gave me a long lecture on how stupid I was to be playing with a heavy piece of lead when I had so many other toys to play with. Dr. Krogh was famous for giving lectures and was always telling other people how to bring up their children. In due course my toe healed, but my nail never grew back properly and all through my life I have had a deformed big toe nail which now, in my old age, gives me a lot of trouble to cut. I must say it has always been a nuisance to me, but only a minor nuisance.

Another thing I loved doing in Tobago was playing under the house and I remember one day finding a lovely nest of soft downy feathers with lots of eggs in it. I was very excited and ran in to tell mother what I had found. She said it must be a duck's nest, as ducks would pluck out the soft feathers from their breast and made a lovely nest with them.

Mother also told me not to go and look at it often, as the duck would get scared and leave all the eggs there and then we would have no ducklings. However, every day I used to creep in quickly to see what was happening and then one day the duck walked out with lots of little ducklings. I was so thrilled and I claimed them as my own. Daddy had a lovely trough made and it was a real joy to see the little ducklings swimming about and flapping their little wings. We used to feed them on cornmeal soaked in a little water and a hard boiled egg finely chopped added to it. This seemed to agree with them as they grew very fast. I'm afraid as soon as they began to grow I lost interest in them and went about my own games.

Every Sunday we went to swim at one of the beaches and there were many lovely beaches in Tobago. Usually on Sunday afternoon we went to see some of mother and daddy's friends, like the Hamiltons who lived at "Green Hill" and always served a sumptuous tea with cakes, sandwiches and lots and lots of other things. Mrs. Hamilton (Dot Hamilton) was a good friend of mother's in Trinidad. She was younger than mother and very pretty and very nice. They had two little boys, Hal and Gordon, both younger than me. The Hamiltons were very well off and lived in a lovely house with a tennis court and a beautiful garden. Mrs. Hamilton's mother, Mrs. Argeroux (not spelled right) was a good friend of my grandmother's, so we saw a lot of them. The grown-ups then played tennis or bridge and the children went to swim in the pool. There was a river running down the side of the hill and there was a little waterfall that gushed into this pool where we used to swim. I didn't like it very much, as the pool had a lot of crayfish that used to give us nips all over our legs and bodies. I always made an excuse and said I had a cold and couldn't swim. The water was also very cold, not warm like the sea.

The "no more pets" vow didn't last too long because the Hamiltons gave me a puppy (much against mother's wish) and we called him Bubbles (*note 6*). He was a cute little fox terrier pup, white with one black eye and another black spot on his body. My father said we would have to have his tail cut so that was the first worry and then soon after that, Bubbles got distemper and mother, Frances and I looked after him. He was very ill and we didn't think he would survive, but he did and then grew up to be a very healthy dog. Bubbles was always with me now and I really loved him. Although he often got into trouble chasing people's fowls and attacking dogs much bigger than himself, the whole family loved him.

We also visited the Kernahans who lived at "Bon Accord". Mr. Kernahan managed the estate for Baba Cipriani until Baba Cipriani went bust (bankrupt) and then Gordon Grant & Company took over. During those visits, we usually went for a swim at Pigeon Point, which was a beautiful beach with lovely calm water, but the only trouble was that there was a big swamp behind it and there were always lots of mosquitoes and sandflies.

There were lots of other places we used to visit, but I can't remember them all. I do remember Friendship Estate, which belonged to Mr. Elton Miller. He lived there with his daughter. Friendship was a beautiful place, they had converted an old sugar mill into a house and had added a long living room and a pantry and kitchen. The Millers were very wealthy people. They were Americans and he had been head of the tobacco company in Trinidad. They had beautiful things in their house, silverware, cut glass and beautiful mahogany furniture. They also had a lovely garden with rose arbors, lawns and flower beds. Mother and daddy enjoyed the Millers' company and often went there, but I didn't like going very much as there were no children to play with and I would get very bored.

As I write and think back, I wonder what happened to the Millers. I expect they went back to America. Years later, when I was married, my husband and I used to go to spend a week or two at Friendship Estate and then it was quite different, just a holiday house with old furniture and lots of peacocks and some horses. I never dreamt when I used to go to Bon Accord and Friendship that one day my husband would be attorney for Gordon Grant and he would often have to go to Tobago to visit these places which Gordon Grant had taken over.

The beach we went to most often was Bacolet Beach, the nearest beach to our house. After church on Sunday morning we would go there for a swim. It was usually very rough and a bit murky. One Sunday morning, one of the policemen from the brass band that had come to Tobago to give concerts was swimming with some of the other band members when he was attacked by a shark. Marie Henri de Verteuil, who was also swimming, went to his aid when he shouted out and dragged him into shore. However, his two legs had been bitten off and by the time he was taken to hospital, he had died. I didn't see this, thank goodness, as when my mother realised what was happening she brought us to the car and told us not to move.

Marie Henri de Verteuil was given a medal for great bravery and she certainly deserved it. After that we very seldom went to Bacolet again.

Mother loved Mount Irvine beach and so did we all. It was usually lovely and calm and the water was very clear. Sometimes we had a picnic and lots of grown-ups and children would go there for the day and bring chicken pelau, potato salad, macaroni and cheese and lots of fruits; oranges, portugals, mangoes etc. Mount Irvine was a coconut estate, so we would eat under the coconut trees. I don't remember who it belonged to in those days, but it was one of the estates that belonged to Gordon Grant when my husband was attorney for them.

Another beach we used to go to was Store Bay, which was beautiful and clear. However, sometimes it could be very rough, with a dangerous undertow, and the grown-ups wouldn't let the children swim. So as you can see, there were lots of lovely beaches where we spent many happy hours and where I learnt to swim very well.

Now my reminiscing brings me back to Gertrude Watson who taught me. She was a good teacher and made our lessons interesting. Daddy was the first one to introduce me to books and now Miss Watson continued the good work by introducing us to good books. Every day she read to us for half an hour from one of the classics. The first one she read to us was David Copperfield, and I remember I couldn't wait for the time to come when Miss Watson would say "alright, children, put away your books, I will read to you now". She read us many books. Ivanhoe, Little Dorrit, Jane Eyre, but my favourite was always David Copperfield. My father and mother were very fond of Gertrude Watson and she often came over to the house in the afternoons and sat with mother and daddy out on the lawn.

When she left the Sorzanos I was very sad and we all missed her. Fancy I never heard of Gertrude Watson after she left, that is, until I came to live in Antigua many, many years later, when one afternoon Phyllis and Arnold Branch (two dear friends of Archie and I) rang to say they were coming to visit us and would be bringing a friend called Gertrude, who used to be Gertrude Watson. I was now about 70 and couldn't believe I was going to see Gertrude Watson again after all these years had passed and not knowing what had happened to her.

As you can imagine, it was really lovely seeing her again and she remembered all the things that I did. She even remembered Monica's and my birthdays. Incredible! She also remembered Aunt Anna saying "Gertrude, never marry a poor man, because when poverty comes through the door, love flies out the window and would you believe it, Thelma, I married a very poor person, but love never flew out the window". Gertrude said she still heard from the Sorzano girls at Christmas.

I will always think of Gertrude Watson as one of the best teachers I ever had. She made school so interesting. When Edris, Stella and Zena were sent to school in Trinidad, Miss Watson left the Sorzanos and Norma, Ianthe and I then had to go to Miss Clark's (Donald Clark's sister). She was a nice enough person and had received a good education in Barbados, but school was not as enjoyable as it had been with Miss Watson.

While we were in Tobago my grandfather Gray died. My mother was very sad and I felt I should be very sad too, but I was too young to really remember my grandfather too well. After he died, grandma and Aunt Anna came to stay with us in Tobago and they spent quite a long time with us. While they were here with us, Aunt Anna prepared Ianthe Guppy (who was a Catholic) and I for our first Holy Communion. I remember it well, the priest who gave us our First Communion was called Father McDonnell and he knew the family well and always called Aunt Anna, "Auntie Ann".

I seem to have forgotten to mention anything more about Ivy Hughes. Well, she stayed with us for quite a while and she gave mother a lot of trouble. First she had a very bad rash and the doctor said she had to have hot baths, which meant that mother had to bring in a big bath pan into the bedroom and fill it with hot water and Ivy had to soak in that. This was a real performance and it had to be done every day. Then, no sooner had she got over that, than she sprained her ankle and had to hobble about with a stick and her ankle all bandaged up. All this was extra work for mother, so instead of her helping mother, she had to be looked after. My father got fed up with all this and told mother Ivy would have to go back home and I quite agreed with him (little as I was). Also Ivy was always protecting her complexion and wouldn't go out during the day unless she had on a long-sleeved and high-necked dress, gloves, and wide hat with a blue veil.

She was really quite a caricature and a laughing stock. Daddy used to say "Ivy, who are you protecting your skin for, the grave?" Anyway, Ivy left and everyone was relieved, my mother most of all.

After we had been in Tobago for about six months, I had a really bad attack of malaria and mother sent for the doctor. He was a Chinese doctor called Dr. Tsoi-a-su (I don't think that's the way to spell it).

When he arrived I had a very high fever and my mother told him about my malaria and how she treated it with quinine. Dr. Tsoi-a-su said "Mrs. Seheult, that will cure the present attacks, but it will not cure her of malaria, so instead I would like to give her an injection of quinine." When I heard that I really started making a fuss and said I would hide under the bed. I was very afraid of being given an injection. Mother was also upset and wished daddy had been there. Finally the doctor calmed me down and gave me the injection, which did hurt quite a lot. He said I would have to have two more with a week between each. I didn't like the idea at all, but realised that although it hurt, it wasn't as bad as I had imagined. I thank Dr. Tsoi-a-su every time I think of it, because from then on I never got malaria again. The thing that used to bother me a lot were my tonsils, which the doctor said were infected and should come out. My tonsils also affected my ears and I got very bad ear aches that were really painful. Anyway, I only got these maladies from time to time, but it was very worrying for my parents.

As I mentioned before, Aunt Anna and grandma came to stay with us after my grandfather died and were with us for quite a long time. Mother was pregnant and she very much wanted her family with her. It turned out just as my mother had feared, my father was drinking much too much and spending a lot of time at the men's club in Scarborough. Mother was very worried about this and naturally was glad to have grandma and Aunt Anna with her. Aunt Anna was great at helping her with baby clothes and clothes for Monica and me. Also, she generally helped around the house. Grandma was her consolation and she always felt that grandma would understand how she felt. At my young age, I didn't worry much, but didn't like daddy drinking, and I didn't like to see my mother so sad. I think life in Tobago changed my mother; she was never again the same happy, carefree person that she used to be.

Then mother had her baby, mother and daddy were looking forward to having a son. It was a baby boy and he died at birth—his name was Augustine. His death was a great sorrow for my parents and for all the family, but for my mother especially. She was very bitter over how the doctor had handled the birth. The doctor's name was Dr. Thwaites and he was very drunk when he was called to the house and didn't know what he was doing, and the nurse who mother had hired from Trinidad to attend to her had stood by and done nothing. The whole family felt her anguish and helplessness in such a situation and I am glad that mother had grandma and Aunt Anna with her at that time.

While Aunt Anna was in Tobago, there was an Englishman called Mr. Link who was in charge of the Government Farm and he wanted to marry Aunt Anna; but Aunt Anna said she couldn't marry him as he really wasn't her class, he wasn't a real gentleman and he was a cockney. I wonder if Aunt Anna would have been happier married to him? He did have some money of his own besides his job, and he was good-looking elderly man with a ruddy complexion, very blue eyes and curly graying hair. I think that Aunt Anna was too old to change her way of life and would have missed all the family very much, having always been so much a part of it. I think my grandmother was very happy she didn't marry him, as she depended so much on Aunt Anna, they got along very well together and I never heard them quarrelling, although I am sure they must have had their disagreements.

The Meadins left Tobago and the Pantins came to live next door. They were 'Boy' and Cathy Pantin. Mother liked Cathy Pantin. The Pantins had five small children, the eldest was about six and the youngest were twins. The three eldest, Basil, Tony and Maureen, were often at our house as we lived so close and mother often gave them lunch with Monica and I.

Dr. Thwaites also left Tobago and I am glad he did as mother wouldn't have him in the house and I don't know what we would have done if we had needed a doctor. It was Dr. Krogh who took his place. Mother and daddy had known him in Trinidad. His sister Lucy was married to daddy's brother Robert. We saw a lot of him and his wife. He married a Miss Blanc, sister of Dr. Blanc. Dr. Krogh liked our house and told daddy "when you leave Tobago, I am going to apply to the government to get this house. It is much more suitable for a doctor as it is closer to the hospital." Daddy replied "I don't mind what you do when I leave, but you won't get it as long as I live in Tobago!" Our house was a much nicer house than the doctor's and was in a much nicer spot right on a hill. After you went by our house, you passed the Sorzano's house, then further up the hill

Victor Collins, Violet Sorzano's younger brother who was killed in the WWI

Violet Sorzano with one of the Urich children

was the hospital, and then past the hospital was the Bell Tank and then further up a little steep incline and you were at the Old Fort and the Lighthouse where one got a wonderful view overlooking Bacolet and Scarborough and lots of other parts of Tobago.

Frances, our nurse, used to bring us up to the Fort Hill most afternoons and there we used to meet our friends and play all sorts of games in the old ruins, running along the old walls surrounding the Fort. The walls were very wide and easy to climb up on and run along them. I'm sure mother would not have approved if she had known. We also used to climb up the lighthouse ladder in the middle of the lighthouse and watched the lighthouse man light the light at six o'clock, it was all a lot of fun. There was also a path leading from the Fort down a grassy hill to a sort of cave which someone told us was Robinson Crusoe's cave, it had a rocky opening and was rather dark inside and I didn't really like going there very much, but it was creepy and exciting at the same time for us children.

Arima

The Arima Train Station

When daddy was transferred back to Trinidad I think both my father and mother were glad. I know my mother was particularly pleased as she had not been happy in Tobago. I, on the other hand, was excited to be going somewhere new. There were a lot of us returning to Trinidad: daddy, Carrington, Frances, Monica, I and Bubbles. And so we had come to the end of our four-year stay in Tobago.

When we got back to Trinidad, daddy, Carringon, Frances and Bubbles went on to Arima, but mother, Monica and I stayed with grandma and the rest of the family in Port of Spain for a few days. Grandma had left Gordon Street

Horseracing in the Arima Savannah

after my grandfather died and Aunt Muriel, Uncle Jack and Uncle Harry had taken a house in Stone Street, while grandma and Aunt Anna stayed with us in Tobago. The funny thing is that I don't remember the house in Stone Street at all, although I was so much older than when I stayed at Gordon Street, which I remember so well. Although I do remember that for the few days we stayed in Stone Street, the Grays came and it was lovely seeing Ena, Joy and Phyllis, Cora etc. Uncle Jack would bring us to the place that the fishing boats came in and we really used to enjoy seeing all the boats sailing into the harbour and all the merchants waiting to buy their fish.

A few days later daddy came to meet us and we left for Arima and to quite a different phase of my life.

Our house in Arima was very nice; not as big and roomy as the Tobago house, but nice enough. Mother and daddy liked it. It was situated facing the Arima Savannah, where they had horse racing, cricket and football matches and other sports. There was a big grandstand and it was always filled with people when they had races. On one side of us was the Arima hospital and the doctor's house. The doctor who was there when we first went to Arima was Dr. Rodriguez and he had four daughters. I can't remember the name of the eldest, but the other three were Carmen, Ignez and Cora, all a lot older than me. On the other side of us was the tennis club, where everyone collected in the afternoons to play tennis.

It was a very French community in Arima. Near to us lived the family of Joe de Gannes and they had a lot of children. The one I was friendly with was Eliane,

La Chance

she was a very nice little girl and we got on well. Then, near to Doctor Rodriguez' house, lived Eliza de Gannes with her three children Ena, Gaston and Rita. Ena was much older than me. The one I played with was Rita, although Gaston always came and played tennis and other games with us.

Then there were the de Gannes that lived past the railway station at "La Chance". La Chance was a lovely big old house with beautiful rose gardens and large orchards of oranges, mangoes and lots of other fruit. They had a lot of children. We often went down to La Chance to play, as they had big savannahs and a little stream at the back. We liked to go up into the large garret, it was full of bats and I was terrified of them, but that didn't stop me. Another thing we used to do was chase and catch butterflies. I always let mine go, I hated to kill them and thought it was awful. The boys would tease me about it and laugh at me, but it didn't bother me.

The de Verteuils also lived closeby. They had three children, Esme, Betty and Claude. Esme and Betty were around my age and Claude was more Monica's age.

Then there were the Harragins, this was the first time I remember meeting them. Uncle Bertie Harragin was my mother's first cousin and as his father had died before he was born. Aunt Clemmie, his mother, lived with grandma and Aunt Anna, so Uncle Bertie had grown up with my mother and they were very close.

Uncle Bertie and Aunt Rosie (Uncle Bertie married Rosie Green from St. Augustine) had three children, Lorna, Josephine (Josine) and Fred. Lorna was older than I was, Josine was my age and Fred was a little younger. Fred's birthday was the same as mine, the 31st August. Naturally, as we were related, we saw a lot of the Harragins, and Josine was my closest friend in Arima. As Josine was also very friendly with Eliane de Gannes, we three were usually together.

The Harragins lived at a house called "El Carmen". It was quite far from where we lived at the other side of Arima. It was a big house with a stone gallery all around it and very large grounds with lots of mango trees. There was a river that ran close to the house (I think it was called the Santa Rosa River, but I am not sure of this) and there was a nice little pool where we swam and spent a lot of our time. We would also go for walks along the banks of the river, which was lovely and shady with a lot of bamboo, and our walk would take us to the Ice Factory where we always went in to see them making the ice. The man there would give each of us a lump of ice to suck on as by the time we reached there we were very thirsty.

Camilla de la Bastide lived quite near to the Ice Factory and we often went to see her. She was more Josine's friend than mine. She was a very pretty girl with a lovely complexion and had lovely thick hair that she wore in two long plaits that fell to her waist. She always dressed in a very old-fashioned sort of way. We wore short skirts and blouses, and she wore long dresses with long sleeves and a high neck. She was an only child and lived with her mother and father, grandmother and great-aunt, and didn't mix with the other children in Arima like we did.

The time we lived in Arima were very much my tomboy days. I was outdoors all day, playing tennis, going down to La Chance and romping about, and in the afternoons playing in the Savannah. Eliane and Josine did the same thing and we only went home for meals. Josine often spent the day with me as her house was so far away. Our parents never seemed to worry very much about where we were, as long as they knew there were a lot of us together. Those were the days of no violence and everyone was very peaceful, and it seems to me that everyone was much happier and carefree than they are in these modern days. How I wish my grandchildren could know a little of those carefree days. There wasn't a lot of money around and all my friends had very little money, and though I suppose their parents worried, they never showed it. None of us had very many toys. Once we had some marbles and a kite we were all very happy.

Grannie Harragin, whom we called Aunt Clemmie, lived with Uncle Bertie and Aunt Rosie and she was very 'hipped' on her health and everyone else's. She was always telling mother I was too thin and that I should wear a big hat as I had too many freckles. I used to hate when she came to the house, because for days after, mother would try and fill me up with porridge and give me Kepler's malt, which I hated. I really didn't eat a lot in those days, but I ate so many fresh fruit that I'm sure that kept me healthy; for now that I didn't get my bouts of malaria anymore, I kept very well, seldom getting coughs and colds. My tonsils did worry me sometimes, but my ears never bothered me like they did when I was in Tobago (I think it was all that swimming in the sea that had affected my ears).

I spent a lot of time at Josine Harragin's house. She had a lot of books and as my love of books never lessened, I often used to get immersed in a book and Josine would get very annoyed when I wouldn't play outside with her, or perhaps bake cakes or make fudge and sugar cakes with her. One thing I hated was cooking, and Josine loved cooking and hated reading, so in that way we were like 'chalk and cheese'.

Monica, my sister, was still too young to gallivant all over the countryside with me, and I'm sure she must have felt a bit left out. I was about ten or eleven when we lived in Arima and Monica was five.

The Ken Gordons lived in Santa Rosa, a village close to Arima. They would come to play tennis and bridge nearly every afternoon. We all liked the Gordons, they were very nice people. Sally Gordon walked with a limp, but I don't know why. Ken was always full of fun and all of us children loved him. They used to have lovely children's parties at Santa Rosa and we all enjoyed them. The grown-ups came too and while we played all sorts of games, they played bridge or just chatted with each other.

I liked Viva de Gannes very much. She was Eliane's mother and I was often at their house. She was so nice to me, and although I didn't realise it at the time, I found out later on that the de Gannes used to have a lot of money, but had lost all their cocoa estates and were now very poor. Joe de Gannes was a lawyer but he never seemed to do very much, and I expect they lived on the little he earned which wasn't much. There were lots of children in that family. André, the oldest boy, Miriam, the eldest girl, Joe Jr., Cyril, Carmen, Eliane, Leon and Thelma. Thelma was the baby of the family, she was younger than Monica.

Leon and I both had very quick tempers and we were constantly quarrelling and fighting. I am happy to say Leon grew up to be a very nice man and had a good job, even though the only schooling he had had was from someone coming to their home every morning to teach him.

I met Leon years later when I was in Tobago staying with our daughter Gillie and her husband Doug at the Crown Point Hotel. Gillie had just given birth to a son, Skene, after having a very difficult time, eventually having to have a caesarean operation, which resulted in serious complications after the birth. Archie and I were in England at the time and had flown out on a day's notice to be with Gillie. Leon and his wife had come to see Gillie as they lived in Tobago and knew Gillie and Doug. Leon said to me "Thelma, do you remember how we used to fight and quarrel in Arima?" I said I certainly did.

Fortunately, most of us grew up to be sensible human beings, at least I hope so. It was nice meeting Leon after so many years and he was a nice man and so was his wife.

I now had many new friends in Arima and all the friends I had made in Tobago I never really saw again. But that's how life is, one moves on and life changes and one makes new friends. However, a lot of the friends I made in Arima I had for most of my life.

I think I must say something about Uncle Bertie, as he was so close to my family, and from the Arima days I was close to him as well. Uncle Bertie was a nice-looking man. He was tall and slim with graying hair when I knew him. As a young man he had been an excellent athlete and had won all sorts of prizes for long jump, high jump and pole jump and had been a very good cricketer. He had captained the West Indies against England in England, and as he was known to be fair and just, he was a great favourite with all his men. After he was married and had three children, war broke out and he joined the West India Regiment and went out to Egypt and Palestine. There he won the D.S.O. for bravery. He was quite a hero when he came back to Trinidad and as you can imagine his mother, Aunt Clemmie, was very proud of her only son and child. The whole family was very proud of him. He was a nice man and liked by everyone, however, Uncle Bertie liked to tease me and Monica quite a lot when we were little girls in Arima. I remember I used to get mad as of course we could never answer him back and in that way I thought it unfair of him to tease us.

Harragin Family: Uncle Bertie, Josine, Lorna, Clementine Collins Harragin (Aunt Clemmie), Aunt Rosie with Fred.

Another thing I really enjoyed when we were in Arima was the cinema. I had only been to the cinema a few times in Port-of Spain when we stayed with grandma, but then I only went with grown-ups. In Arima we all went in a big group of friends. The cinema was just across the Savannah and we would all walk across it and go to the matinee, which started at 4 o'clock in the afternoon and ended about 6 pm. We would buy peanuts and during the interval (there

Violet Sorzano, Emily Seheult, Carmen,me, Marie Sorzano, Monica Seheult at Cronstadt down the islands (1929)

was always an interval in the middle of the film) we bought snow balls, shaved iced dipped in a sweet syrup, which they sold outside the cinema.

Those were the days of the silent films when someone played a piano all through the film. We always went to the serials which continued on the Wednesday. We used to love the serials: "The Perils of Pauline", "The Clutching Hand", Eddie Polo in the "The Bull's Eye" and many others. They always stopped at a very dramatic moment, someone hanging from a cliff, usually the hero, the clutching hand just about to grab the heroine and so on, so of course we couldn't wait to see the next instalment.

Another favourite activity we loved was going to the races. The de Gannes or perhaps it was the de Verteuils had a race horse called "Kitty Gill", and of course we all backed Kitty Gill to win. I remember all of us shouting "come on, Kitty Gill, come on!" but I'm afraid I don't ever remember Kitty Gill winning. We would all go into the Savannah with our cars, there were about fifteen or more cars and we (that is the grown-ups) used to get up little sweepstakes amongst ourselves at a shilling a chance and the prizes were, 1st, 2nd & 3rd, and one often won $25.00 to $30.00 which in those days was quite a nice sum of money to get. The grown-ups often took chances in the big sweepstake at the grandstand as well. Race day was always a gala day in Arima and all the owners of the cars that went to the Savannah brought nice teas and 'goodies' so that we were all well fed at tea time. Of course we children bought a lot of things from the vendors in the grounds, hot peanuts, snow balls, peppermints and lots of other tasty treats.

I have forgotten to mention that when we went to live in Arima, daddy bought a new car. It was a six-seater, as it was called in those days, and it was very roomy and comfortable compared to the little Ford two-seater we used to have. We often went into Port of Spain to see grandma and family on a Sunday. We either spent the day or went in about two o'clock to have tea and spend the afternoon.

The Arima house had a big kitchen and two nice servants' rooms outside. Carrington and Frances had the two servants' rooms, but I cannot remember anything about the cook, she certainly never made an impression on me whoever she was.

Carrington and Frances were now part of our family. We always felt we could go to them if we were in trouble or worried about anything. Once, when Frances had taken a holiday, mother got someone to be there with us when she and daddy went out. One night they went to dinner with the Ken Gordons and this foolish woman who stayed with Monica and I began to tell us all sorts of stories about jumbies and la jabalas who walked about at night and dealt with the devil, and that she was afraid to go home after six o'clock because she had to pass by the cemetery, and after dark that is when the jumbies used to be flying around the cemetery like balls of fire. By this time, Monica was terrified, I told her that it was a lot of nonsense as I had often passed the cemetery at night and had never seen any such thing. I really wasn't afraid, but then I was eleven and Monica was only six. Monica wouldn't go to sleep until mother and daddy came home and then went to sleep with them in their room. Mother sent the woman packing the next morning and we were all glad when Frances came back from her holiday. She never told us foolish things like that.

There was another family in Arima that we were friendly with, there were the Canon and Mrs. Merry and their four sons Jack (he was away at school in England), Cyril, Harry and David. Cyril was older than I was and didn't mix with us very much. Harry was about my age and he was always one of the crowd.

Horseracing in the Queen's Park Savannah

David was much younger and didn't mix with us at all. Cyril was tall and strong and nice-looking, but we all thought he was conceited. Harry wasn't very tall and he was thin and plain with sticking-up hair like pins and rather projecting teeth, but he was very nice and we all liked him a lot.

Both Cyril and Harry went to Queen's Royal College in Port of Spain and it was a very long day for them as they had a long way to walk from their house to the railway station where they had to catch the 7 o'clock train. When they arrived in Port of Spain they then had to take the tramcar to Queen's Royal College. They didn't get back until late in the afternoon, and then had to walk home, so we really only saw them on the weekends. Jack came back from school in England just before we left Arima. He was a very nice young man of about seventeen.

Now we come to going to school. Mother decided to send me to the Arima Convent. I really don't remember much about what I learned there. In fact, I really don't think I learned much. The nun that taught us was Mother Dominic, she was old and always reminded me of an owl. She used to wear big round glasses and had a rather hooked nose, and sitting up there on her rostrum she looked like a big owl staring down at us. It is a good thing I had a good grounding in reading, spelling, addition, subtraction etc. from Miss Watson and Miss Clark, because I really don't remember learning anything at the Arima Convent. I also don't know where all the other children I played with went to school, they didn't go to the Convent, perhaps their parents got someone in to teach them, that certainly would have been better for me than the Convent. Josine, Lorna and Fred went to a Miss Beckles and I'm sure she was better than Mother Dominic.

One of the other things I really enjoyed when we lived in Arima was going down the islands with Mr. and Mrs. Ken Gordon. They went down the islands every year during the summer holidays to a bay at Monos called Domos. It was the last bay on Monos and a lovely place. The house was very big, with a very large stone gallery, a dining room and a big drawing room downstairs, but we spent most of the time on the big stone gallery which had two hammocks and lots of deck chairs. Upstairs was a long gallery and about five bedrooms leading off the gallery, with a lavatory upstairs and a bathroom and lavatory downstairs.

The Gordons asked Eliane, Josine and I to stay with them for two weeks at Domos and it was a wonderful holiday. Josine got homesick after a couple of days and she went back home, but Eliane and I had a wonderful time. We would get up early in the morning to see the boatmen pulling the seine. We would run down to the beach in our pajamas and the boatmen (about four of them) would be hauling a little seine to catch sardines and Jack fish for bait for Mr. Gordon and his brother Stuart and anyone else who was staying there, when they went fishing. It was exciting hearing all the boatmen speaking in patois and saying if it was a good catch or not. Sometimes they would catch some small sharks which they would keep to eat. Once they caught quite a big shark and when they cut it open, there was quite a big fish in its stomach. They used to catch all different kinds of fish and what they didn't want, they threw back into the sea and it made me happy to see the fish swimming away.

After seeing the seine pulled we changed and got some oranges and 'portugals' from the pantry and sat on the jetty sucking them until Mrs. Gordon called us in for breakfast. The rest of the day was passed swimming, rowing a small boat around the bay—not going to far from shore—climbing the hill behind the house and picking and eating sugar apples. There were a lot of sugar apple trees up the hill and at that time of year, the fruit were all ripening. We used to pick a lot for Mrs. Gordon as well.

The Gordons had three small children, Nancy was four, Ken was about three and Hamish, the baby. We spent some of the day amusing Nancy and Ken.

The Gordons also had friends who came down for the day or for two or three days, so the house was always full and bustling. As the Gordons had a lot of servants, Mrs. Gordon always seemed to have a lot of time to swim, go in the boat and play bridge. It was really a lovely carefree time for Eliane and I. When they asked me to go again the following year, Monica protested vigorously and said she wanted to go too, so Mr. Gordon said , "well, let her come, if Thelma will look after her". So she came with us the next year and she thoroughly enjoyed it, and really wasn't much trouble at all.

While we lived in Arima, we visited grandma and the family who now lived in Longden Street, which they preferred to Stone Street. As usual we enjoyed our stay with them and saw a lot of the Grays. It was when we were in Arima that the Grays decided to go to live in England. Aunt Lottie's sister lived there and she sent the money for them to come to England. All the Grays were very excited at the thought of going to England, but grandma was very distressed as she knew that once they went she would not see them again, which of course was the case. Everyone was very busy getting clothes made for the whole family. Aunt Anna sat at the sewing machine all day and Ena, who was the eldest, with Aunt Anna's guidance, had learnt to sew quite well, was a great help. So between Aunt Anna and Ena, they got a lot done. Mother also helped when she could. I wasn't happy about the Grays going away, they had always been my good friends from the time I was a little girl. Phyllis and Joy had spent lots of holidays with us in the different places we had lived. When the Grays left Trinidad, we all went on board the boat to see them off, but grandma didn't go and mother stayed with her. I missed them very much when I went to stay in Port of Spain with grandma and Aunt Anna and they weren't there.

After I got married I went to England with Archie, and we went to see them. Ena was engaged (I didn't like him). Joy was married and had two children, Phyllis wasn't married, but Cora was and she was expecting her first baby. Uncle Willie had died and Aunt Lottie was very much the head of the family. I really enjoyed seeing them again. But I'm afraid I never saw them again after that visit. They had all married and gone their separate ways and when I was in England, we spent most of the time in the country and never got around to seeing them before we left. I regret now that we didn't make the time. One always thinks there is lots of time, and that the next time we made a trip to England we would make the effort to go and see them, but somehow it never works out that way.

While we were in Arima Dr. Rodriguez left and Dr. Wupperman came to live there. Dr. Wupperman and my father were very good friends so we saw a lot of him and his wife. They got married late in life, but they had three small children when we were in Arima and after we left had two more I think.

Mother was happy to have a good doctor living near to us. While we were there, there was a bad outbreak of typhoid fever and the hospital was full of typhoid cases. Dr. Wupperman came over to the house one day and said "Emmie, you will have to be inoculated against typhoid, as you live near the hospital and flies can carry the typhoid germs". So we all had to be inoculated and Monica and I got fever and felt very badly for about two days, but I'm sure Dr. Wupperman was right to make us have the inoculation and my mother was very glad that he had made her aware of the urgency of being inoculated.

St. Joseph

Me and Monica with our parents and Bubbles. In background St. Joseph Public School, convent is to the right (1927)

Well, life went on happily in Arima and then daddy was transferred once more, this time to St. Joseph. I think mother and daddy had been happy in Arima and were a bit sorry to leave, but it was a promotion for daddy and it meant that we would be nearer to Port of Spain and could get there quite easily by train, as there was a very good train service from St. Joseph. Also daddy would have to go into Port of Spain quite often to the head office and mother could go in with him to see the family. The houses in Siparia, Tobago and Arima were all government houses, provided for the District Engineer, but in St. Joseph there was no government house, so daddy and mother went to St. Joseph beforehand to see if they could find a suitable house to rent.

They found one which belonged to Frank Gransaull and took it. It was right on the top of the hill and had a nice view, but it wasn't a nice big roomy house like the ones we were accustomed to. To get to it, you left the Eastern Main Road just by the Police Station and went up a steep hill, then past the St. Joseph Catholic Church, then turned right at the first turning after the church, then after a short distance, one turned left and next up another steep hill and then turned left again and went up another short steep hill and there was our house at the top of the hill on the road going to Maracas valley. Once more I had to leave all my friends in Arima and knew that in S. Joseph I would find new ones. It wasn't the same excitement leaving Arima to go somewhere new. I was getting older and I suppose I wanted to feel more settled.

The whole family and this included Carrington, Frances and Bubbles left Arima and went to St. Joseph. Mother and daddy soon made a lot of friends and then I did too. Just across the road from us lived the Huttons. They lived in a big house very high from the road in the front and in a very commanding position with a lovely view overlooking the Caroni plain.

The Huttons had five children. Pearl, who was married to Frank Austin; Jack, the eldest son who was away in Costa Rica, then Eric, Littie and Terrence who all lived in St. Joseph and went to school at Queen's Royal College.

Then there were the Farfans who lived quite near to us, and by taking a short cut through the boy's school, I could get to their house in five minutes. Mrs. Elfie Farfan had known my mother when they were young girls. Her husband Emmanuel worked at a government office in Port of Spain and went to work every day by train as he didn't have a car. There were six children in the Farfan family, Sheila, who was my age and grew to be my best friend, then Godfrey, Jocelyn, Martin, Monica and Albert. Jocelyn was friendly with Monica.

Then there were the Agostinis, who had seven children. The eldest, Joe, worked in Port of Spain, then there was Doreen, Rosemay, Olga, Elsa, Kathleen and Theresa. I was most friendly with Olga, but was also friendly with Doreen and Rosemay, even though they were older than I was.

There were lots of young people of around my age. The Boos boys, who came from St. Augustine; the Thavenots, who also came from St. Augustine; and the three Pasea girls from Tunapuna. So, as you can see there were always lots of children around my age (I was 12 years old when the family moved to St. Joseph).

During the holiday we always collected at the Farfan's house, which was a nice big house with nice grounds, and Mrs. Farfan was always glad to have young people around. The Farfan's house was very close to St. Joseph's Convent and near the Roman Catholic Boys School; it also overlooked the tennis court. It was a nice tennis court and we children played tennis there when no grown-ups wanted it.

Terrence Hutton, me, Sheila Farfan and Littie Hutton at St. Joseph tennis club

My life in St. Joseph was quite different to my life in Arima. I was now becoming more grown up, I was getting to the flapper age, and I began to think more about my looks! I felt I was too thin and wanted to put on some weight. I wanted my hair to begin to curl and most of all I wanted to get rid of my freckles. Mother said she would give me some cream to put on my face at night, and told me to keep out of the sun. I began brushing my hair a lot and setting it after I

St. Joseph

bathed, and I tried to eat more but never felt very hungry. So my hair began to curl and the freckles began to fade, but I still didn't put on much weight.

In St. Joseph mother began to play a lot of mahjong and she really enjoyed that. She organised a ladies four, Mrs. Farfan, Mrs. Hutton, Mrs. Gransaull and herself, and they went to each other's houses in the afternoons and played mahjong. Daddy would play bridge with Mr. Hutton and some others and sometimes he would play mahjong if the ladies couldn't get a four together.

Daddy had an office in St. Joseph quite near to the St. Joseph church. He went there about three times a week, and into Port of Spain head office the other days. It was while we were in St. Joseph that Carrington learned to drive the car. Carrington was very nervous at first, but eventually got accustomed to it, and he was always a very slow and careful driver which was a good thing. Now he could take mother, Monica and me where we wanted to go if daddy didn't feel inclined to do so.

Monica and I went to St. Joseph's Convent, which was right next to our house. I am afraid the teaching there was almost as bad as it was in Arima. At least the arithmetic was. Mother Patrick taught us arithmetic; she was old and getting a bit senile and we really never learned a thing from her. The girl who sat next to me in class was Malia Gonzales, and she was very good at arithmetic and used to explain the sums to me. Mother Lydia taught us history and literature and she was not too bad. However, we didn't stay at St. Joseph's Convent long; mother decided to send us to Holy Name Convent in Port of Spain, so we went to board with grandma, Aunt Anna, Aunt Muriel, Uncle Jack and Uncle Harry who now lived at Cipriani Boulevard. I don't know why mother decided to send us to Holy Name Convent instead of St. Joseph Convent in Port of Spain, but I think it was because she thought that it would be nearer for us to walk to Holy Name from Cipriani Boulevard.

I was a bit nervous of going to a big school like Holy Name and felt that I wouldn't know anyone there, but it wasn't as bad as I expected, even though everything and everyone was very new to me and I felt a bit lost at first. The nuns and the girls were all very nice and after a couple of weeks Monica and I settled down.

I was happy boarding with grandma. I had been with them such a lot in my life that I felt very much at home and very loved. There were some nice girls in my class. I got friendly with Barbara Newbold and with the two Archibald girls, Phyllis and Kathleen, and lots of others whom I liked a lot.

The nun who taught us most subjects was Mother Thomas, she was very severe but she was also very fair and just. I liked her a lot. Then there was Mère Guinevere who taught us French; Miss Lamie who taught us literature and last of all Mère Raphael who taught us arithmetic. Mère Raphael was a brilliant mathematician and she couldn't understand how I didn't understand what she was trying to teach me. I did alright with the straightforward sums like fractions etc., but when it came to problem sums, I was completely at a loss. I didn't like Mère Raphael very much and I expect she thought I was a bit dumb. Another teacher that we had was Miss O'Connor. She taught us geography and she was a good teacher and I learned a lot from her.

Monica and I would wake up early in the morning and get dressed in our school uniform, which was a pleated navy blue skirt, a white blouse and a striped tie. Under our skirts we had to wear navy blue bloomers, the same colour as our skirts. We also wore a panama hat with a ribbon around it in the same colour as our ties. We were always supposed to wear our hats in the street, but all of us carried our hats in our hand until we got close to Holy Name and then put them on. Holy Name Convent was opposite the Memorial Park and quite near to the Savannah. It was just next door to the Holy Name Church where, every Friday afternoon, we went to Benediction. Mère Rosamins would go around clapping her hands saying "Benedicte, Benedicte, everyone put on your hats and come along now." Mère Rosamins taught us singing and I'm afraid she really didn't think much of my voice, so I wasn't chosen to be in the choir, but I did join in with the others when they were singing the Benediction hymns.

After Monica and I were dressed and had our breakfast, we would walk to Holy Name. We usually met other girls on their way to school and we all walked together, speaking about our homework and discussing it with the other girls.

Sometimes we walked around the Savannah, but usually we walked to school by Tranquillity and through Dundonald Street and by the Princes Building and then through the Memorial Park. On the way we met Claire and Petite de Verteuil, the two Gianetti girls, Bianca and Angela, and then further on, Yolande de la Bastide. Yolande was in my class, so we exchanged views about the homework. Petite was in Monica's class, Bianca was in the class above me, and Angela in the class below me.

When we got back to grandma's in the afternoon, I never really wanted to go out again. I loved having a bath, changing into a comfortable dress, and settling down to doing my homework or often to reading a book. I used to like to get my homework finished before dinner, then after dinner I would sit in the front gallery with grandma and Aunt Anna and play my mandolin and wait for Vierra's ice cream to pass. Aunt Anna would always give me money to buy one, they were so delicious. Ice cream doesn't taste like that nowadays.

Then I joined the girl guides. I was persuaded to join by Sheila Farfan, who said it would be lots of fun and we could get badges for passing different tests. I wasn't too sure about this, but Sheila was so keen and mother and Aunt Anna thought it would be a good thing for me to do. So I did join and went to guides every Monday afternoon. I used to catch the tram car and then get off at the Botanical Gardens where the guides had their hut. Miss Burslem was the head of guides and she was always there. Our patrol was called the Hummingbirds and our patrol leader was Lynda Knaggs.

Sheila and I were in the same patrol. I soon found out that although guides meetings were every Monday afternoon, we were expected to take tests to get different badges and this meant going again on a different afternoon during the week quite often, and also on a Saturday morning. I remember getting three badges. A cooking badge!! Swimming and life saving badge (this was good fun as we would go to the swimming pool at Government House to practice, and Major Knaggs used to come and teach us the different strokes for swimming and lifesaving.

Then when it was time to take the test, we went down the islands to St. Mary's Bay for the day. There were a lot of us and we all brought our own lunch and Major Knaggs was the one who judged us. I got very good marks for this and came first. After a year of girl guides, I had had enough and so had Sheila and we both left after explaining that it was too inconvenient for us as we lived in St. Joseph.

Another good friend I had at school and at guides was Jean Richards. I was also friendly with her sister Delci, but as Jean was my age and in my class, we had more in common.

My friends at school and my friends in St. Joseph were completely different, and I was much friendlier with my St. Joseph friends. The weekends in St. Joseph were always fun. We went home on Friday afternoons and returned to Cipriani Boulevard on Monday morning. Carrington met us at school on Fridays and brought us back to school on Monday morning.

Every Sunday there was a market at St. Joseph just above the church on the hill, near to daddy's office, where there were vendors selling fruits, vegetables and sweets. We would all go and my parents would give Monica and me sixpence to spend while we were there. We would come home with all sorts of fruits and delights such as halla and lavinie, a lovely tasting sweety which was home-made with all different flavours, peppermint sticks some of which had a lemony flavour.

After the market, we all collected at one of our houses and played mahjong, or went down to the little river at the back of the Farfan's land for a swim. The water wasn't deep, but it was cool and clear, and the sun shining on the water made it that much more inviting. In the afternoon, a whole crowd of us collected by the Agostini's house and as that road was a dead end, we used to skip rope and play different games like hopscotch.

Every Sunday morning we all went to church at St. Joseph Church, which was a lovely old church. It was low mass and it was usually over in 3/4 of an hour. After mass, sometimes we went to Scott's pool to swim. Scott's pool was in Maracas valley and we all walked there as we didn't have cars to bring us. We always enjoyed the walk as there was practically no traffic, just a few donkey carts, a man riding a bicycle, and an occasional motor car (*note 7*).

Bubbles always came with us and he was a great nuisance, chasing chickens and ducks and getting into fights with other dogs. All my friends would protest vigorously and say "Thelma, why do you bring Bubbles?" But I couldn't leave him at home, he really loved coming with us. Sometimes I would lock him up at home, but usually half way to Scott's pool we would see Bubbles coming down the road to meet us.

It was called Scott's pool because the pool was on old Mr. Scott's property. He lived on the opposite side of the road on top of the hill with his daughter Josephine. It was a lovely, deep, clear pool and we had permission from him to swim in the pool whenever we liked. (Mr. Scott and Josephine very seldom used it). There was a little pavilion with a thatched roof, and benches where we would eat if we spent the whole day. There was always a lot of us there on a Sunday—the Hutton boys, Sheila and Godfrey Farfan, some of the Boos boys and Monica and I. We always brought some snacks to eat and had a happy morning. But we never liked the walk back home, we were tired and it was hot.

On Sunday afternoons I often went to the cinema with Mr. and Mrs. Hutton, Littie and Terrence. The Empire was the best cinema in Port of Spain and it was a thrill going to see the films, which were silent in those days. Gary Cooper was my favourite film star and I liked Ronald Colman as well. I also liked Greta Garbo and Babe Daniels, and many others whose names I don't remember. It was very good of Mr. and Mrs. Hutton to take me with them, but I expect it was really Littie and Terrence who persuaded them.

Every Sunday morning, the Huttons had a bridge morning and Mrs. Hutton would make lovely homemade ice cream and some tasty meat pies and sandwiches. Daddy usually went and mother did sometimes, but as mother didn't play bridge, she usually preferred to stay at home. If we didn't go to the river, Terrence would usually ask me over to have ice cream and often Sheila came as well and we would play ping pong on the nice ping pong table which they had under their house.

Eric Hutton got a motor bike and there was great excitement, he asked me to go for a ride on it on the pillion. I thought it was great and we rode all over St. Joseph, uphill and downhill. However, when I got back home, daddy was very angry and told me I must never do that again as it was very dangerous. Eric asked me again the next day and reluctantly I had to refuse and tell him that daddy wouldn't let me go. I didn't like Eric Hutton very much, but I did love going for a ride on his motorbike.

When we went to live in St. Joseph I was twelve years old, and was very much a tomboy. Now, as I was getting older, I began to leave my tomboy ways behind. I remember the first time I saw Archie, my future husband, we were all skipping outside the Agostini's house which was near to the tennis court. Four young men walked off the court, one was Johnny Agostini from St. Augustine who stopped to say hello to us. The other three were students from the Imperial College of Tropical Agriculture. Joe said, pointing to Archie, "that is McDonald, he is a very good tennis player". I was very attracted to him from that moment, but Joe went on to say "he is very friendly with Pearl Austin", so I just put him out of my mind. However, I always remember the first time I saw him, I was just turning thirteen and know he, who was six years older than me, just saw me as one of the crowd of young teenagers.

Above: Me, Doris Seheult and Sheila Farfan St. Joseph (1925)

Right: Leo and Emily Seheult, me, Monica, and Bubbles (1926). Below Leo & Emily's home in Carmody Rd., St Augustine.

Marie Sorzano, Sheila Farfan, me, Eliane de Gannes, Eliane Seheult at Cronstadt down the islands (1929)

Monica Seheult, Eliane de Gannes, me, Sheila Farfan, Eliane Seheult at Cronstadt (1929)

An Expedition to Mount St. Benedict

AN EXPEDITION WE often went on was a walk to Mount St. Benedict. We all enjoyed this very much. We would set the alarm to ring at 5 o'clock in the morning and as soon as it rang, we would get ready very quietly so as not to disturb mother and daddy (although they knew we were going to Mount St. Benedict).

We drank a hot cup of cocoa that Frances had prepared for us, and as soon as it started to get light, we would all meet at the bottom of our hill and set off past the presbytery of the St. Joseph Church, and take the very steep hill between the presbytery and old Mrs. Gransaull's house. (Mrs. Gransaull lived in a lovely old house with her son Ray, his wife Emmie and their little daughter who was handicapped.) From there we went past the Bovell's house and all the way along the back of Curepe, past the St. Augustine Club and the Cotton Station houses and then up through the little village until we got to a gate and a pillar marked PAX and the beginning of the road to Mount St. Benedict. We didn't take the road, instead took a well-trodden path which was a shortcut to the "Rest House". It was a lovely walk, all of us together, beautifully cool with the dew sparkling on the grass. We watched the sunrise and listened to the early morning sounds, cows mooing, cocks crowing, birds chirping, families waking up and getting ready to go to work.

When we got to the Rest House, we saw Stella Seheult who ran it, and each paid a shilling and got bacon and eggs, toast and a big cup of chocolate. The Rest House was a wooden house. As you entered, there was a living room with comfortable chairs and holy pictures on the wall, then there was a passage with

Road to Monastery, Mount St. Benedict

bedrooms on either side (not many rooms) and at the end of the passage was a dining room where the guests ate, and that is where we had our breakfast. After we had breakfast, we thanked Stella, who was a tiny, thin person with graying hair drawn back from her face in a little bun at the back of her head, and then went up to the church to say a short prayer.

The Church was a wooden building on high pillars. It had a big cross in the front and it was bright and cheerful inside and quite small. Afterwards we went to see Brother Maurins (he was a Maingot) and Dom Placide (he was a Gauntaume), both Trinidadians who liked to see us young people. Brother Maurins was in charge of the bees and took us to see the beehives. He wore a big hood over his head and long gloves, and he would be covered with bees. It was very interesting and the brother collecting the honey always gave us a bottle to share between us. I never liked honey, so didn't take any, but the others enjoyed it. Afterwards we walked up as far as the reservoir, but we never went as far as Mount Tabor which was above Mount St. Benedict and overlooked the Caroni plain on one side and a deep valley on the other, giving one the sense of being on top of the world.

The monks had built the road up to Mount St. Benedict and all the buildings, the guest house, the church and the monastery where they lived. Brother Gabriel, who was a great big man with a long red beard, was the one who designed the

Noviciate House, Mount St. Benedict

Mount St. Benedict

Garden, Mount St. Benedict

Cloister, Mount St. Benedict

View from the bridge on Monastery, Mount St. Benedict

Mount St. Benedict

buildings and was the main one who did all the work on the road and buildings. Everyone loved Brother Gabriel, and even when I was grown up and married, he was still working hard at Mount St. Benedict. Now of course all this has changed, there is a two-storey guest house, a huge abbey and on the way up to Mount St. Benedict is a seminary where young men go who want to become priests.

It is all very magnificent now, but I still prefer the little rest house and the little wooden church that we used to walk to from St. Joseph, and it was all most enjoyable. Again, we didn't like the walk back home, which was hot in the mid-day sun. However, that never deterred us from going back often to Mount St. Benedict.

I always associate St. Joseph with Mr. and Mrs. Frank Gransaull, who lived at the bottom of the hill going up to our house. They were about my parents' age and had no children, which was a great grief to them. They were fond of me and often used to call me in if I was passing their house. Mother and daddy liked them a lot and they played mahjong together. Frank's mother and his brother Ray and wife Emmie lived further down the hill from their house. Mrs. Gransaull was a very petite, dainty old lady who spent a lot of her time in church. Ray and Emmie did not go to church at all and neither did the Gransaull's other son, Eddie Gransaull. This was a real grief to the old lady, and I think that is why she spent so much time in church praying. We all liked Ray and his wife and felt sorry for the sadness in their life over their daughter who was handicapped and whom they loved very much. Her name was Manuela and she died when we still lived in St. Joseph. Both Ray and Emmie were inconsolable and Emmie said to me "Thelma, now you will have to be our daughter". I often went to see them, but when we left St. Joseph , I seldom saw them again. Ray died quite young of 'creeping paralysis' and Emmie left Trinidad and went back to her family in Canada.

Old Mrs. Gransaull had other daughters, Mrs. Arthur Murray was one of them. She was a very beautiful woman—called Manuelita (which means 'little Manuela', which was old Mrs. Gransaull's name) and they lived in St. Augustine.

While we lived in St. Joseph there was a Miss Miller who played the mandolin very well and gave lessons. She lived with her mother and two sisters near St. Joseph's church. Sheila and I decided that we would like to take mandolin lessons from Miss Miller and our parents were glad for us to do so. My father bought me a nice mandolin and Sheila got one as well, and we went to her house for lessons twice a week. I really enjoyed playing my mandolin, and when Miss Miller moved from St. Joseph to Belmont in Port of Spain I continued taking lessons from her and went by tram car after school. I caught the Woodbrook tram and then transferred to the Belmont tram, which stopped quite near to Miss Miller's house. The mandolin gave me such pleasure and I used to play it for my own entertainment. I wonder now why I didn't continue, I would never have been a very good player but it would have continued to give me pleasure. My father used to play it well by ear, and I envied that he could just pick it up and play the songs he knew. I, on the other hand, always had to play with a music book and learn the pieces by heart. I often wonder what became of my mandolin, it just seems to have vanished, funny—I never even asked about it.

We sometimes took the train from St. Joseph and went to visit the Paseas. Mrs. Pasea, the mother of Ailsa, Gemma and Brenda lived in Tunapuna. She decided that she was going to put together a couple of 'acts' for a concert they were having in San Fernando and she asked Sheila and me if we would like to be in it. So after getting permission from our parents, Sheila and I agreed and would go regularly to Tunapuna to practise.

There were five us, the three Pasea girls and Sheila and I. We had to do a Japanese dance called "Gay little girls from Japan". We were dressed in embroidered kimonos with a wide sash and a big bow at the back, slippers and chrysanthemums in our hair. I cannot imagine anyone less Japanese looking than I was with my blonde hair and freckles. Then we did "Three little maids from the Congo"! Also, Ailsa, Sheila and I had to recite a poem called "The Discontented Husband". We had to go down to San Fernando for the weekend and spend it with Dr. Lasalle. We went down on Friday afternoon, did a rehearsal on Saturday morning at the Concert Hall, and the play was Saturday night. The concert was quite a success and the place was crowded. Our acts received encores and so did my recitation. We were certainly very proud of ourselves. Mrs. Pasea had accompanied us and we all came back on Sunday afternoon.

All this time we were all getting older and very much more conscious of boys and had crushes on different boys at various times. All the Hutton boys had a crush on me and out of them I liked Terrence the best. He was a really nice boy. Then I liked Werner and so on, and so on, it was all very innocent. We would sometimes have dances at the Farfans and sometimes at the Huttons and sometimes the Boos boys would invite us to their big house in St. Augustine. Mr.

Boos died while this big house was being built and Mrs. Boos and all her children moved into it when it was finished. Mr. Boos didn't leave much money when he died and it was hard on Mrs. Boos as she had nine children (eight boys and one girl) to take care of and they were all still in school. There were Carlson, Oscar, Werner, Haydn, Neville, Elsa, another boy whose name I can't remember, Sydney and Pat.

The Boos house was just opposite the St. Augustine Club and we used to enjoy going there. Carlson and Joe Agostini were older than all of us and they would teach us how to dance. So by the time I was fifteen, I could dance quite well.

Me with Bubbles

Another family in St. Joseph was the Gomez's, who lived opposite the Frank Gransaull's (Mrs. Gransaull was a Gomez and a sister of Neen and Margaret who lived in that house with their father Mr. Gomez). Then there were the other Gomez's who lived further up the hill nearer to the Huttons. There were eight in their family but all much older than I was, except for the last two boys, Herman and Ralph. The two Gomez families were not related to each other. The children in this family were Marie, Agnes, Hector, Herwald, Doris, Audrey, Herman and Ralph. Agnes and Hector lived in the States and only came back to Trinidad occasionally. Sometimes Doris and Audrey came to the house to play mahjong with the grown-ups and the other boys kept very much to themselves.

One day I noticed Herman following me when I went to the Farfans, and I began to worry about it and it made me a little nervous. One afternoon, when it was just getting dark and I was coming home from the Farfans by the short cut, suddenly Herman appeared out of no where and grabbed hold of me and tried to kiss me. I was really scared, and got away from him and ran as fast as I could into our house. I didn't want to tell mother and daddy, so I told Frances. She said "Miss Thelma, never walk home when it is getting dark by yourself, always get one of the others to walk home with you." Well, after that, I always followed her advice and I noticed that Herman wasn't following me around anymore. Years later, I heard that Herman had become a bit peculiar and I felt sorry for him and the anguish this must have caused his family.

Audrey Gomez got married to a Mr. Macaulay from Esperanza Estate. Audrey was very pretty and everyone liked her. All of us teenagers went to St. Joseph's Church to see the wedding. Mrs. Gransaull played the organ in the choir and she asked me if I would like to go up to the choir loft to look on. I asked if Sheila could come and she said yes, so we had a good view of the whole wedding. My parents were at the wedding and so were Sheila's. Audrey looked very pretty. After Audrey got married Doris went to the States, and Marie was left at home to look after the family. Herwald died of tuberculosis and Ralph, the youngest boy, got it too, but they sent him away in time and he recovered.

Marie in the later years of her life turned very peculiar. She got engaged to a man called Ernest Eckle, but after they were engaged for a few months, she told him that when they got married they have to be like St. Joseph and the Virgin Mary. Ernest said he was not prepared to live that way and he broke off their engagement. Marie took him to court for breach of promise, but the case was thrown out. It was after this that Marie became even more peculiar. She really didn't have an easy time of it, as her father in his old age married a girl of seventeen and this was a terrible shock to his children.

When Archie and I were in our middle years and lived in Carmody Road, St. Augustine, the Macauley's built a house right opposite to us and came to live there so we saw a lot of them. They had four children, three daughters who were married and a son Lawrence who inherited the house when his father and mother died.

Well time was going on and Sheila and I were now fifteen years old. I was spending the day with Sheila and she told me that she had fallen in love with a boy, or I should say a young man, in Port of Spain called André Cipriani. She said they met every day when she was going to the convent, and André was going to St. Mary's College. Sheila said "Thelma, this is not a crush, I am really in love, André is coming over tomorrow and he is bringing his best friend, and I want you to come over". Naturally I said yes as I was very curious to meet André.

The next afternoon, when I went over to Sheila's house, André was already there with his friend Nicky Marquis. I liked them both immediately and I know both liked me and we had a lot of fun together. After that Nicky would come every week and Sheila told me that Nicky really liked me a lot. He was a nice young man and I liked him too.

One afternoon when André and Nicky came to St. Joseph, we decided to go for a walk to the St. Joseph reservoir. To get there we had to pass our house and mother saw us walking past and came out to speak to us. Sheila introduced mother to André and Nicky, and I could see mother was annoyed about something, but I didn't know what it was. When I got home later that afternoon, mother said she was surprised at me getting friendly with a Portuguese and I was not to go around with him again. I was very annoyed about this, as Nicky was one of the nicest boys I had met and he was clever and ambitious. Anyway, I didn't listen to mother and continued seeing Nicky.

Sometimes Sheila, André, Nicky and I would go to the pictures and Nicky would ride home with me on the tram car and drop me at grandma's. Nicky also often rode his bicycle as far as Holy Name Convent and walked home with me. He didn't do this often as he was studying hard for exams and often stayed late at St. Mary's. I liked Nicky a lot, but I wasn't in love with him, the way Sheila was with André Cipriani.

One afternoon André (who had just won the scholarship and had broken off with Sheila as he was going away soon and felt it was no point in keeping up their friendship), came to the house on Cipriani Boulevard to see me. We talked for a long time and he told me that he couldn't continue to stay involved with Sheila. He then asked me if I was in love with Nicky because if I wasn't, I should stop seeing Nicky as Nicky was very serious about me, and he was not concentrating on his studies, and he, Nicky, probably could get a scholarship if he studied harder. I then told André I wouldn't see Nicky again as I was much too young to be serious about anyone. I know Nicky was very upset by the whole thing, but I didn't know what else I could have done.

There was a girl called Consuelo Lazzari who was very much in love with Nicky and as she was very pretty I don't know why Nicky didn't like her. I never saw Nicky again until after he had won the scholarship and he came to say good bye to Sheila and me. I know Sheila was very heart broken at André breaking it off with her, and I suppose Nicky was very hurt at the way I treated him, but I broke off with him for his good, and because I was too young to be serious about anyone.

Sheila and I were at the Hutton's house one Sunday morning playing ping-pong with Littie and Terrence and having some of Mrs. Hutton's lovely homemade ice cream, when two students from the Imperial College of Tropical Agriculture came over. One of the students was a young man called Sheffield and he came downstairs to play ping pong with us. He was a very young student. I think he was taking the diploma course. The following weekend, Sheffield came to St. Joseph again and Littie called to invite me over, so I went. Then Sheffield, his first name was Leo, began to send me short letters, asking me to go to the pictures with him. I said I couldn't. I wasn't at all attracted to him so didn't want to give him any ideas that I may be interested in him. Anyway, he soon got tired of asking me out and I didn't hear anything more about him. Later on, through Leon de Gannes and his wife, I heard Sheffield had married Leon's wife's sister and lived in England where they had a lovely home and were very happy.

One day, while we still lived in St. Joseph, mother decided to cut her hair. She had lovely long hair and would put it up in lovely bun at the back of her head. It suited her and I used to love to see her brushing her hair at night and plaiting it into two long plaits to go to sleep. My father also loved her long hair, so you can imagine the consternation in the family when we got home one afternoon and found that mother had cut her hair. Daddy was very upset and I was too; with short hair, she didn't seem like mother. I don't know what made her do it, probably she saw all her friends with their haircut and thought it would be nice to be in the fashion as well. However, I don't think she really liked it either and it wasn't long before she decided to grow it again and we were all so delighted.

I remember Aunt Rosemay coming to stay with us after her husband Uncle Freddie had died. He died of a heart attack when he was middle aged and it left Aunt Rosemay and the children very bereft. Aunt Rosemay, her daughter Odette, and her younger son Karl stayed with us for a month, while Yves, her eldest son who worked in Port of Spain (I think he worked for Archer Coal Depot) found a house for them to live in. Odette started to take lessons in shorthand and typing and when she was through, got a good job. Karl went to St. Mary's

Aunt Rosemay Seheult, née Seheult, Yves, Karl and Odette Seheult.

College where he did very well. He was clever and a brilliant mathematician and got the Jerningham gold medal* for Maths. He could have got a scholarship but he didn't want to continue at school, he wanted to leave to get a job and help his mother. Karl was a good-looking young man, but he was very short, about 5 ft., and got teased in his young days and he began to drink too much and this worried his family. Anyway, I am glad to say he soon stopped drinking and got a scholarship to go to America and study electrical engineering. Eventually he rose to be the head of the Telephone Company and then the Electricity Company. He was very good at his job and highly thought of by everyone. He was completely honest. So Aunt Rosemay saw all her three children do well in life and they continued to love and support her as long as they lived.

Unfortunately, Odette died of cancer of the lungs at a young age (she was a very heavy smoker) and Yves died in his middle years of a heart attack, so now Aunt Rosemay only had Karl left. Aunt Rosemay was still alive when Archie and I left for England in our later years, but as we never returned to Trinidad, we never saw her again. Yves lived in England and died soon after we arrived, so we went to his funeral and I was so sad thinking of Aunt Rosemay and how much she must be grieving in Trinidad.

In the telling of Aunt Rosemay and her family, I seem to have strayed from St. Joseph, but they were very nice people and wanted to mention them as I liked them very much. Karl eventually married a 'petite' girl, and they had one girl, Suzette, who was very pretty, she was the apple of Karl's eye.

* Hubert Jerningham KCMG DL. In June 1897 he was appointed serving until December 1900. While he was Governor, the Trinidad Government Railway was extended from Cunupia to Tabaquite. The railway junction formed by this extension was named 'Jerningham Junction'. He also instituted an award for the top student in the Island Scholarship examinations, a gold medal called the Jerningham Medal (today known as the President's Medal). Wikipedia.

During the time we were in St. Joseph, grandma and Aunt Anna never came to stay with us, but saw mother very often, as Monica and I boarded with them during the week, so they saw us all the time. Uncle Harry, Aunt Anna's brother, often came to spend the weekends. He would come by train on Saturday morning and go back with Monica and me on Monday morning. He really enjoyed his stays with us and as he had such a dull life, I was glad to think of him enjoying his weekends.

One weekend he came to us and was very excited. He had drawn a horse in the sweepstake and it was the favourite to win. The name of the horse was "Guykapura". It was a Venezuelan horse and it was the best. Everyone told Uncle Harry that he almost had the money in his pocket as he was sure to win. If he

Monica Seheult (1930)

won, he would get $10,000; which in those days was a lot of money. Uncle Harry told us he was in such a state of excitement he couldn't stay in Port of Spain or go to the races, as he felt the suspense was just too much for him. So it wasn't until Sunday morning that Uncle Harry found out that Guykapura hadn't run at all. At the last moment the owner had pulled it out. Poor Uncle Harry, the disappointment he felt was awful.

He was a poor man and he had made plans to buy a house (in those days you could get a very nice house in Port of Spain for $4,000) with a nice amount left over. The whole family felt very sorry for him. It turned out that someone had bribed the owner of the horse to pull his horse out of the race.

Ever since then, if you drew a horse in a race, you never knew the name of the horse until you had won the 1st, 2nd or 3rd prize. I must say, our family never seemed to have much luck where money was concerned.

An Excerpt from my Diary

My godmother Camillla Siegert, née Chipchase, wife of Louis Siegert, the youngest of the three Siegerts, sons of Dr. Siegert who came to Trinidad in 1860s.

THE STORY ACTUALLY STARTS with Matilda Hughes' seventeenth birthday. She had two sisters, Eliza and Charlotte, called Liza and Lotte by their family and friends, and her very young brother Frank who was only about four and whom Matilda loved like her own little boy.

Albert Collins was very much in love with Matilda (called Matty), but was a great deal older than her. He asked her to marry him on the night of her birthday party, but said he had something to tell her and didn't know if she would marry him after he has told her what it was. He confessed that he had an illegitimate child, of about 3 years old, a little girl. He had had a brief affair with a coloured girl who used to come to do his mending for him. She was a very beautiful girl and encouraged him, and he did not resist her. However, it was all over now for the last two years, and since then she had married a man of her own standing and he never even saw her or the child for whom he had no love, although he did support the child.

Matty was very disturbed at this news, but as it was all finished with, she said it really had nothing to do with her as he didn't even know her in those days. So Albert and Matty were married about a year later. Matty grew to love him with all her heart and she was his precious love whom he could barely leave out of his sight. They were very happy together, but not very well off. Matty had their first baby after ten months of marriage. She had a normal delivery, but Albert was almost demented with worry over her, and felt he never wanted another child. The child was a boy and they called him Frederick and then after that, the babies came at regular intervals: after Freddie came Clementine, then Norah, then Harry and after many years Anna.

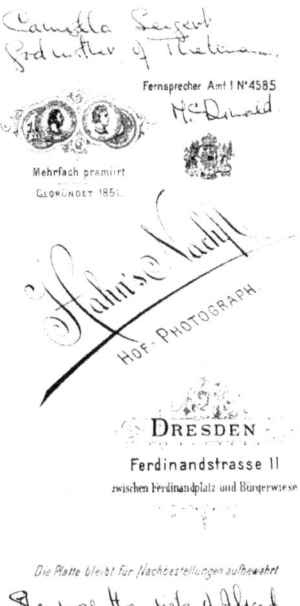

Matty had two good friends, Rosina de Montbrun and Anna Waterman. Rosina married a very rich French Creole, Raoul Sorzano. He was many years older than Rosina, but as Rosina was rather plain and poor, she married him without hesitation. Raoul was an unattractive man, short and fat with a bald head and a growing paunch, but Rosina made him a good wife. She didn't love him, but she was always grateful to him for having married her and given her all the luxuries of life.

Rosina went on many trips to Europe and Raoul showered her with gifts of jewelry, but as she grew older, she became more and more mean, and although she professed to love Matty very much, she never so much as gave her a sixpenny piece. Rosina was Anna's godmother and she gave her $5.00 for her birthday and $5.00 for Christmas, but that was as far as her generosity went.

However, she never failed to send for Matty if any of her children or Raoul were ill, and Matty never failed to leave whatever she was doing to go to help her. This annoyed Albert, who greatly disliked Rosina and Raoul, which was really because he greatly resented the things Raoul could give Rosina, the trips to Europe, the beautiful jewelry, which he would have loved to give to his beloved Matty, but was unable to. Matty knew this and tried to show him in every way that she would rather be married to him without any money, than to anyone else.

Rosina and Raoul had four children—Arneaud, Rosie, Phillipa and Gustave. Gustave died when he was very small. Arneaud grew up to look exactly like his father, Rosie and Phillipa were very plain, but they were very witty and amusing and also clever and talented with their hands. Rosie made a good marriage and was very happy, Phillipa married a tall handsome man who had a great deal of money and charm but no sense and soon went through most of his money. He drank too much and eventually committed suicide. Both Rosie and Phillipa grew up with Matty's children Clementine, Norah, Harry and Anna.

Matty's other good friend was Anna Waterman, who also married a very wealthy man called Matthew Chipchase. Anna was not beautiful but she was a very striking woman, tall and slender and walked like a queen. She was very proud and quite the opposite to Matty in disposition, but she truly loved Matty, and would have given her gifts of money, but Matty would not take it, so Anna always contrived to send her parcels of luxuries which she knew Matty could never afford.

Anna had one daughter, Camilla,. She was a plain-looking child, much to her mother's disappointment, as she was proud and vain and, as Camilla was her only child, she had hoped she would be beautiful and talented. So she made Camilla walk for 1/2 an hour morning and afternoon with a book on her head, until she walked like a princess. Then she had to practice the piano for two hours every day. Camilla was also given elocution lessons until she spoke quite beautifully and with great expression, and every afternoon Camilla had to go out with her mother to sit with her friends, sitting quite still and made to bow and smile politely to all Anna's friends. By the time Camilla was thirteen, she was a most accomplished girl. She could play the piano beautifully, although rather mechanically. She could speak French, Spanish and German fluently and danced most gracefully.

When Camilla was fourteen, her parents sent her to a finishing school in Paris. And when she returned home at seventeen, the "ugly duckling had turned into a swan" and was a real beauty. Her best friends were still Matty's girls, Clementine and Norah. Anna was a good deal younger than they were, so wasn't as friendly.

Camilla married one of the richest men in Trinidad, of the Siegert family and of German descent, who was charming but rather vulgar. Anna had made this match for her; she was still completely dominated by her mother. Camilla was the perfect hostess and ruled their beautiful home with great grace and charm. Their house was noted for the beautiful balls and everything was most lavish. The food was delicious, they had a French chef from Paris, their house was magnificent and their gardens were a real show place with its fountains and lawns and flower beds. Camilla liked this life, it was what she had been trained for, but there were lots of people who said she was not faithful to her rather fat German husband. If this was true, no one could ever really know for certain, as she was most discrete.

Camilla had one great sorrow: she had no children. She made the great mistake of her life when she adopted a daughter of a cousin of hers called Viola de Craine. She did everything for Viola and she forgot her old friends; instead she showered all her attention on Viola. Her money, her fabulous jewels, were all for Viola, her every thought was for her.

Sadly Viola was a shallow girl who had no love for anyone, and when she got older and found out that Camilla wasn't really her mother, taunted her with it, saying "why should I listen to you, you aren't my mother—I don't love you." This broke Camilla's heart, but she admitted it to no one, not even to Clementine or Norah who still continued to see her often.

Then the great blow came when the Siegert company went bust, and Camilla was left with very little money. She had to move out of her beautiful home, and moved into a small house which was very nice and comfortable, but to Camilla after her palace, it was a cottage. She took the news of the disaster with great fortitude but what really affected her was that Viola could no longer live in the lap of luxury. Viola also never failed to tell her so, and eventually Camilla's mind retreated into a world of its own and she no longer spoke, but just sat in her high-backed chair, with her beautiful gown and her hair exquisitely done up and never spoke to a soul.

Christmas was a Time I Loved

On Christmas Eve in St. Joseph we all went to midnight mass. We would walk to church as it was so close. It was lovely walking in the cool, sparkling night air, with the sky full of sparkling Christmas stars and the Church bells ringing out a joyous welcome. The church looked so beautiful, all lit up with candlelight. The choir sang Christmas hymns and after mass everyone met and embraced wishing each other a happy Christmas. It was something I will never forget.

Before lunch, everyone liked to collect at the Huttons for lovely Christmas snacks and drinks, and by the time Christmas lunch was served at our house, everyone was in a gay and happy mood. When we got home, there was always freshly baked ham with hops bread and pasteles, and everyone was happy and joyful. Christmas Day all the family came from Cipriani Boulevard and we had a lovely big Christmas lunch which mother, Frances, and the cook had been busy all Christmas Eve morning preparing.

First we had pasteles, then we had delicious corn soup, then we had roast turkey and ham, or fricassee chicken for those who preferred it. As side dishes, we had macaroni and cheese, potato puffs, petit pois, fried plantain, and rice. For dessert, there was plum pudding with brandy sauce and mother's baked custard with strawberry jam on top and a fluffy meringue on top of that. Balloons were hanging from the ceiling in the drawing room, the dining room and the gallery.

After lunch, the older people went to have a siesta and we young people went to the Farfans to play mahjong or sit around and talk. And this is how I remember my St. Joseph Christmases.

The Treasury under construction

St. Joseph Bridge

While we lived in St. Joseph, daddy built a big bridge across the river near to the St. Joseph Hill and the Police Station. It was a big bridge; I think it was the biggest in Trinidad at that time. It was a very fine bit of engineering, and there was a big opening ceremony that the Director of Public Works and lots of other dignitaries attended. They took a lot of photographs of the bridge, and we got a large print of one. We were very proud of daddy.

Daddy also built the Treasury building in Port of Spain and it was still the best building in Port of Spain at the time we left Trinidad. My father, with his qualifications and smart brain, should have been Director of Public Works, but he had a drinking problem, which was a great handicap to him as it made him very undependable. However, even so, we were very proud of my father, as he was an honest man and always ready to help anyone in need—in fact this was one of the reasons why he never had much money for himself and his family.

Our life, that is Monica's and mine, continued as usual and we were both happy and content with this arrangement. Monica had a lot of friends and as she loved going out, she was out with them most afternoons. I often went to see my friends and they came over to see me, but to be truthful, I preferred to stay at home and read. I got very immersed in Charles Dickens and as Uncle Jack had the whole collection of Dickens works, I read David Copperfield over again and liked it even more than when Miss Watson read it to us. Then there was Nicholas Nickleby, Little Dorrit, the Old Curiosity Shop and many others, like Ben Hur, Fabriola, Vanity Fair etc. This was one of my greatest joys, to get into a comfortable dress and read. Aunt Anna would say "Thelma, you read too much". But to me, there never seemed to be enough time to read all the books I wanted to read.

At Carnival time, I enjoyed the festivities preceding Carnival even more than the two days of Carnival. The few weeks before Carnival was a time of Carnival parties at different people's houses, it was open house for all the young people.

The Siegerts had a Carnival evening every week and hired a band called 'The Northern Syncopaters". There were so many of the boys we knew in it. There

"We always brought lots of serpentine and confetti and whenever we met a band, we had a fight with confetti and serpentine."

was Leonard Anderson who played the piano, Michael Anderson played the trombone, Raffie Sorzano played the Saxophone and lots of others whose names I don't remember. They were a great band and they were just a little older than I was. We would dress up in any costume we liked. I went as a gypsy, and as a Spanish dancer with mother's Spanish shawl and a rose in my hair. Aunt Muriel used to come with us to see that we behaved ourselves and all our crowd used to meet at our house in Cipriani Boulevard and walk over to the Siegerts who lived in a big house in Victoria Avenue. Other times it was at the Ciprianis, and a few others, but most of the time it was at the Siegerts. I think Aunt Muriel used to enjoy it as well and we never gave her any trouble.

Besides our group, there were lots of other young people from different places and everyone gathered together and met different people and had a great time. At midnight, Mr. Siegert would come out and say to the band "Alright now, play 'God Save the King' and everyone go home now'; and we did. There was never any strong drink served, just sweet drinks and fruit juices and there was never any bad behaviour. If there had been, the Siegerts would have stopped the parties and everyone would have been sorry.

Carnival Monday and Tuesday were the days of going downtown Port of Spain to see all the bands. We would go upstairs of Stephens and watch the bands coming up Frederick Street. We would throw serpentine and confetti, and there were always great things to eat, hot roasted peanuts, ice cream cones and sugar cakes made of peanuts, some coconut, and peppermint. We would stay until about 2 o'clock and then go home, then get ready to go round the Savannah in daddy's car to see the bands in lorries going around the Savannah. We always brought lots of serpentine and confetti and whenever we met a band, we had a fight with confetti and serpentine. This continued until it got dark and then we went home.

I remember Aunt Rosie got up a band with twelve of us, with all girls in it. We were dressed in royal blue velvet tops with three blue gauze frills over velvet skirts, blue stockings and silver dancing shoes. We had blue velvet caps with silver music notes on the front of it and silver music notes on the bodice of our dresses. It was a very pretty costume, and we all went to the Princes building where the big Carnival dance was held. Everyone loved our costumes but our group (band) wasn't big enough to get a prize. We danced all night; at least I did and had a lovely time. Those were the days that one could go to a dance alone and fill up their programmes as everyone went in a crowd, sometimes just boys, sometime girls, one didn't have to have a partner. The dance at the Princes Building was the highlight (Last Lap) of Carnival.

Marie Sorzano would often come to spend the week-end with us at St. Joseph. She was a little older than Monica, and besides being cousins, they were very friendly. We enjoyed Marie's visits and she enjoyed them too, as she was an only child and a bit lonely. Josine Harragin and Eliane de Gannes came to spend weekends with me and as we had so many friends in St. Joseph we always enjoyed ourselves. I would often go to Josine and Eliane's in Arima and it was always nice being with the Arima crowd again, though now it was quite different, being older. I missed Gaston de Gannes and Riba, as they had left Arima and now lived in Port of Spain; instead I saw a lot of the Merry boys who would come over to Josine's house.

The Princes Building

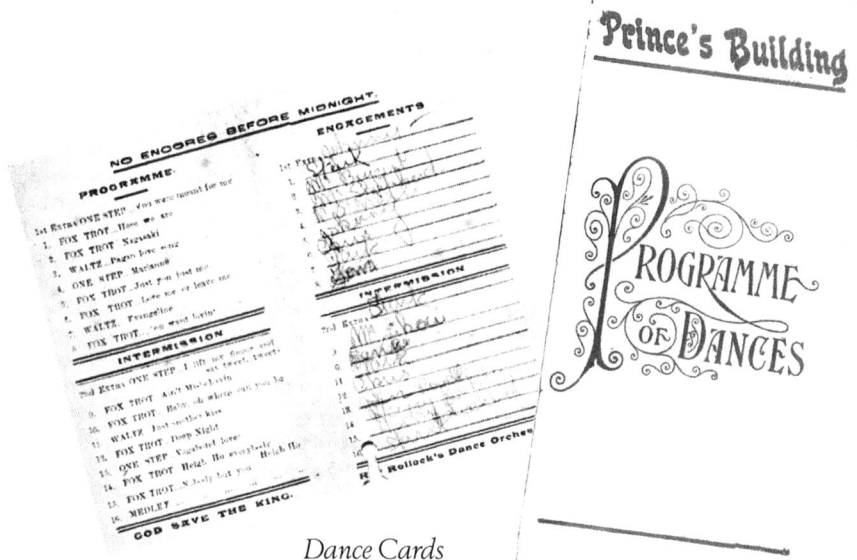

Dance Cards

St. Augustine

Me at age 18

ONE DAY FRANK GRANSAULL came over to see mother and daddy and said that he had decided to sell the house we lived in, but of course he wouldn't sell it until we had found somewhere else to live. So my parents went to look at various likely houses in St. Joseph, but couldn't find anything suitable, so daddy said we should try St. Augustine as Poppa Kerr said that he was sure we would find a nice house there. So once more we were on the move.

I didn't want to leave St. Joseph at all as I had so many friends there, but I did have some friends in St. Augustine and also it wasn't far from St. Joseph. Mother and daddy went house hunting. First they looked at a house in Ragbir Street and nearly took it, but then saw one that they preferred in Carmody Road. I am very glad they took the one in Carmody Road, as I preferred it too. Eventually, I got to love St. Augustine and that is where my home was for nearly the next fifty years of my life, and right there in Carmody Road.

Before we left St. Joseph, the staff of daddy's office, headed by Mr. Mitchell, gave daddy a going-away gift of a lovely Westminster chiming clock and a framed illuminated scroll. It was a lovely present and daddy was very pleased; we all loved to hear the clock chiming during the day. Daddy had been promoted to Executive Officer of the Public Works and his office was in Port of Spain at the head office. We were all very proud of him and felt he really deserved it. And although he was very pleased, he didn't like to go into the office every day from eight in the morning to four in the afternoon. When he had his own district, he made his own hours, which suited him better. Daddy liked Mr. Mitchell a lot and when he was transferred to Port of Spain, he brought Mr. Mitchell with him.

With Monica (1930)

Years after, when I was travelling by train from St. Augustine to Port of Spain with one of my children, I met Mr. Mitchell on the train and he told me how sad everyone in the office was over my father's death and how greatly he was missed. Mr. Mitchell said "he will never be replaced, you know". My father had been dead about three or four years, and he was still very much missed by his staff.

There were also lots of parties for mother and daddy before we left St. Joseph. The Farfans and Huttons gave Monica and I a going away party. I felt sad at the idea of leaving all my friends, for although I knew I wasn't going far, I realised it would never be the same again, with my friends coming to my house and I running over to theirs.

I remember very well the day we moved to St. Augustine. The Public Works lorry bought all our furniture and other belongings and mother, Frances and Carrington were there to receive them as daddy was in St. Joseph seeing that they were all taken and safely packed in the lorry. It was a very busy day and mother had planned that we would have sandwiches and some fruit for lunch, but Mrs. Kerr, Poppa Kerr's wife, sent us a lovely basket of lunch for all of us. It was very welcome and very thoughtful of Mrs. Kerr and we certainly all appreciated it.

During the week, it was the same life for Monica and I as usual, going into Port of Spain to grandma's for the week and going to school. Mother often came down for the day with daddy (who had lunch at grandma's) as she felt lonely in St. Augustine all by herself.

Aunt Anna continued to make my dresses for me, cut my hair and corrected me when necessary. She was like a second mother to me and was very devoted to me. She looked upon me like a daughter and I loved her very much. I used to call her my fairy godmother. I also got into tempers and often said things I didn't mean and then I was so sorry afterwards.

During the weekends in St. Augustine, I still missed my life in St. Joseph. I made new friends of the two Fraser girls, Betty and Toodie, but it wasn't the same. By this time I was growing up and I was thinking more of dancing and boys than I used to. Soon after we left St. Joseph I left school and then I was much at loose ends at first. I helped mother a bit and read a lot and of course met young men, some of whom had crushes on me. I often saw Josine as the two aunts, Sybil and Maud Green, lived in St. Augustine in a big house, called "Hill View" on the Eastern Main Road. Josine often came to spend some time with them and I used to go to see her or she would come over to our house. It was a time of making new friends and going out a lot with lots of different people.

One day, Mrs. Hutton told mother that young Archie McDonald was ill. He was staying at 'Ritchie's Home', and as she felt that he was far away from his own home in Antigua, he would like to see some young people. So mother asked me if I would go and I said yes, as I had seen Archie often and always liked him. So mother and I went to see him at Ritchie's Home, which was a big house next to Tranquillity Club. I think Archie was glad to see me, but rather embarrassed that he hadn't shaved that day. It made me sad to see him feeling so ill and that he had nobody of his own near to him to come and see him, so when I heard that he had gone home to his mother and father in Antigua, I was relieved, as I knew he would be well looked after there *(note 8)*. So for quite a time I didn't see Archie again and went out with my friends and enjoyed my freedom from school.

# My Debut

I HAD JUST TURNED SEVENTEEN, and there was the great excitement of making my debut. Josine Harragin, Eliane de Gannes and I were making our debut at the same time. There was going to be a big dinner at Hill View, where the Greens lived. It was a lovely house for a big party. Aunt Rosie made Josine's and Eliane's dresses, but Aunt Muriel said she was going to give me my dress and she wanted Miss Gomez (who was a very well known dressmaker in Port of Spain) to make it for me.

Aunt Muriel ordered the material from Maillard's store (they sent away for it). It was silver net, a coarse weave and very beautiful. Miss Gomez helped Aunt Muriel and me choose the style. It was the silver net over a very pale pink satin. It was made with a tight fitting bodice and a full skirt with silver frills cut on the bias and the skirt was very full at the bottom but not at the waist. I had a bunch of small pink rosebuds in the front of the dress with pink rosebuds falling to the side of the waist where there was another bunch of pink rosebuds, and then a trail of pink rosebuds falling down the skirt to the hem. It was a beautiful dress, looked simple and fitted beautifully. Miss Gomez was so pleased with the way it fitted and how it looked. She said it was one of the most beautiful dresses she had ever made.

I wore silver shoes and pink rosebuds in my hair. Everyone told me how beautiful I looked and of course I knew I looked lovely and that made me sparkle. I wore a necklace of small crystals that Aunt Anna gave me and they looked beautiful too. (Thelma wore the same necklace on her wedding day. It was later handed down to Robin, her daughter, and has been worn by various family members on special occasions since then.)

So, I had a lovely time at my debut, and could have filled my programme many times over. Josine and Eliane had their dresses made by Aunt Rosie and unfortunately they were not well made. There was wire in the skirts to make them stick out and they looked more like Carnival costumes. Uncle Bertie told mother how pretty I looked and admired my dress. He said Josine's dress was a real failure and he was sad about it. Josine was also very disappointed in her dress and wouldn't go to the big ball at the Queen's Park Hotel.

The Greens (Aunt Rosie's family) gave a big dinner at Hill View and there were lots of people there: mother and daddy, Aunt Rosie and Uncle Bertie, the Cory Davies and lots of other older people. Then there were all of us young people as well as a lot of students from the Imperial College of Tropical Agriculture, but not Archie as he wasn't in Trinidad at the time.

I often wondered as I got older if I ever thanked Aunt Muriel enough for all she had done for me for my debut. She took so much trouble to get everything perfect for me, and spent her own money, of which she had so little. Young people are so thoughtless about things like that. Anyway, I know she was delighted with the result of all she had done, as everyone told her I was the belle of the ball and that gave her great pleasure.

After I had made my debut, I now felt truly grown up and often went to dances at the Queen's Park Hotel, Stauble's Club, and down south at Spring Estate, Pointe-a-Pierre and in San Fernando. I always had a lot of partners and enjoyed myself, but sometimes I liked to be on my own and read a book or do my embroidery. I didn't like to go out that much.

I saw a bit of Betty and Toodie, and we often went to their house to dance after dinner. Students from the Imperial College of Tropical Agriculture would come over as we lived very near the college. In those days I didn't see Archie that often, just now and again, but I always liked him a lot and was always glad when I met him at the cinema and we sat near to each other, or when I went to a dance and danced with him. There were many young men that liked me, and I am sure Archie didn't have any idea that I liked him.

DINNER COUPON

HOGMANAY REVELS.

No. 444

This Coupon entitles holder to one reserved seat for Dinner and dancing afterwards.

Guests are respectfully requested not to interfere with Decorations or throw foodstuff about Dining Room.

This Coupon will be collected by Head Waiter.

Annual Xmas Dance.

Trinidad Northern Rugby Football Club.

Queen's Park Hotel, 7th December, 1929.

Yaille 56—243

VENTURE HOCKEY CLUB DANCE,

IN AID OF THE DEMERARA TOURING FUND.

Music by Northern Syncopaters.

Yaille 60—80

Dance

Programme

	ENGAGEMENTS
1	Maguire
2	
3	West
4	Jack Davy
5	Jack Hutton
6	Vernon
7	
8	
9	Riches
10	Barif
11	Jack
12	Kerr
13	Savary
14	Chris
15	
16	Hurst
17	
18	
19	

117 Franklin 9

Holiday in Barbados

With Emily Seheult, Stanley Evelyn, Vernon, Miss Fletcher and Eric Lange at the Aquatic Club, Barbados 1930

One day, when daddy wasn't feeling very well, he decided we should go to Barbados for a month's holiday. We stayed at the Ocean View Hotel—mother, daddy, Monica and I. When I think of how much daddy paid for all of us to stay there, it seems unbelievable. Something like $400.00 for the month, including all our meals, and such meals they were too!! The food was really good.

The hotel was run by Victor and Edgar Marsden and old Miss Marsden. Victor organised the meals and Edgar looked after the books and Miss Marsden took care of the bedrooms and linen. Of course they also had very good domestic help. The Ocean View Hotel was just outside Bridgetown, right on the sea. There was a small beach where one could swim, but it wasn't very nice, so we usually went down to the Engineer's Pier where the water was crystal clear blue

Ocean View and Hastings hotels

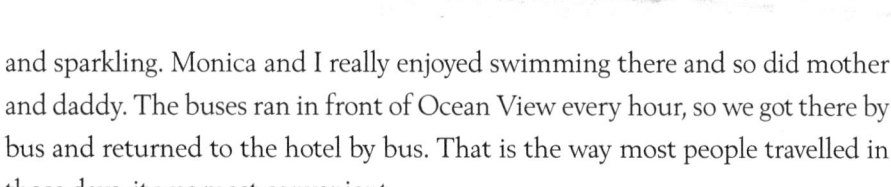

and sparkling. Monica and I really enjoyed swimming there and so did mother and daddy. The buses ran in front of Ocean View every hour, so we got there by bus and returned to the hotel by bus. That is the way most people travelled in those days, it was most convenient.

Mrs. Lange and her son Eric from Trinidad were also staying at Ocean View and mother and daddy knew them well from Trinidad, so we saw a lot of them. A young man called Stanley Evelyn, who had been at the Imperial College of Tropical Agriculture, came to see them very often, and I got to know Stanley very well (I hadn't known him as one of the I.C.T.A. students before). Stanley was always asking me out and I know he liked me a lot but I'm afraid I wasn't at all interested in him as a boyfriend. However, he did bring Monica and me to see a lot of places in Barbados in his little two-seater car. I also went to dances with him at the Marine Hotel and daddy usually came with us.

Sometimes I would go with de Coursay O'Neil and his fiancée, and Tommy Edwards was usually my partner, and I realised they didn't think Stanley Evelyn in their class. The Barbadians were very snobbish. This annoyed me, as I thought Stanley just as good as him.

The "Little Train" at Conset Bay, Barbados.

Twice, we spent the day with Mrs. O'Neil and de Coursay at their lovely old plantation house in the country. We had gotten to know the O'Neils because Murray O'Neil worked at the Public Works Department as a district engineer under daddy, and he had written to his mother to say we were staying in Barbados. There was also a young man called Athol James who was also staying at the Ocean View. He had been very ill and his parents brought him to Barbados to recuperate. He liked me, and I liked him more than Stanley or Tommy Edwards. Athol, Monica and I often went swimming outside our hotel. After Athol left Barbados, I never heard of him again, he looked so delicate so I hope he was alright.

Athol James, Monica and little Hope

Daddy, mother, Monica and I went by the 'little' Barbados train to Bathsheba to spend the day at the Atlantis Hotel. Travelling on this 'little' train was quite a unique experience; it went very slowly, and when one of the passengers' hats blew off, believe it or not, the train stopped for her to go and pick it up. We couldn't understand why the train was stopping in the middle of nowhere, until we saw the woman getting off the train to collect her hat which had blown to the side of the tracks.

Bathsheba was very different to the rest of Barbados, rocky and hilly and the sea was very rough. We all swam in the shallow end of the beach where the waves weren't very big. We saw the flying fish fleet coming in at sunset and it was a most beautiful sight, with the sea brilliantly coloured by the setting sun.

The Horsfords were staying at a house in Bathsheba and they asked us to come and have tea with them. Daddy knew Mr. Horsford well as he too worked at the Public Works in Port of Spain. The Horsfords were Barbadians and always went to Barbados for their holidays, they were nice, simple people.

With Annie Seheult

With Emily and Leo Seheult and Monica

Monica, me, Jenny and Emily Seheult Gray

Joan, Margery, me, Leo Seheult, Annie and Jocelyn

Then mother, daddy, Monica and I went to the Crane Hotel for a day. It was on a bluff and one had to walk down to the beach. The waves were very high and it was a windy, rough day, so we decided not to go for a swim. The Crane Hotel was on the other side of Barbados and tourists liked to go and stay there. I think I preferred the Ocean View, which was nice and central and easy to get about, and also very near to Bridgetown. De Coursay O'Neil signed us up as members of the Yacht Club, but we went much more often to Engineers Pier.

We had a very pleasant month at the Ocean View Hotel and I think it did daddy a lot of good. But no sooner was he back in Trinidad that he started to drink too much again. It made me very sad, as I loved daddy very much and knew that he really would have liked to give up drinking, but could not do so. I think all his responsibilities were too much for him.

As soon as we got back from Barbados, Archie asked me out. We invited some other young people and we all went to the cinema, which in those days was a very nice outing. I then began to see a lot of Archie and really liked him very much, but I was never really sure if he liked me any more than wanting a pretty girl to go out with sometimes.

The Sugar Revue

Around this time, Landy de Montbrun was putting on a concert called "The Sugar Revue". Betty Fraser and Marie Chittzola, who both gave dancing lessons, were helping him with it. Betty Fraser asked me and Sheila Farfan if we wanted to be in it and we both said yes. We all collected at Landy's house to rehearse and got together often. We would have ackra and float with boiled corn for dinner. Sometimes, we went to the Empire Theatre, as that was where the concert was going to be held. It was all a lot of fun, although at times I wished I could just stay at home and read a book and relax instead of rushing off most days to rehearsals.

After the concert in Port of Spain, "The Sugar Revue" went to Barbados to put on a show at the theatre over there. Mother and Mrs. Chittzola came with us as chaperones. We went to Barbados on the *Simon Bolivar,* a Dutch ship. Daddy, mother, Monica and I had previously travelled to Barbados on the *Simon Bolivar,* and I had met the doctor on board and he was very attracted to me. He was a nice man and nice looking, but I thought he was too old for me and I wasn't at all in love with him. He had asked daddy for my hand in marriage and daddy had asked me how I felt about him. I was never so surprised in my life and said I wasn't the least bit in love with him and he was too old (he was probably about thirty years old at the most). So this time I met him again and he was most attentive.

The "Sugar Revue" group stayed at the Marine Hotel, which was very nice, and after the matinee and night show, there was a big dance at that hotel. Stanley Evelyn didn't come to see me this time and I wondered what had happened to him. I think he left Barbados and I heard later that he got a job in St. Vincent.

After a few days in Barbados with the show, we returned to Trinidad on a very dilapidated old ship. It was listing a lot and everyone was afraid to sleep in the cabins, so we all slept upstairs on deck. I know mother was very nervous and was very glad to get back to Trinidad as was I.

After Barbados, Landy took the show to San Fernando, where the cinema was packed. Cecil Hobson was there and as usual, he was very attentive. Cecil was a nice young man with a good job in the oil fields in Pointe-à-Pierre and a good tennis player. He was in love with me and wanted to marry me, but I wasn't in love with him, though I did like him.

```
             Fighting Irene & Two Gun Muller
    - - - - - - - - - - - - - - - - - - - - - - - -

Gather all you people from round di land
And hear how Irene join di hooligan band
This scandal did happen at the Jumby Ball
And the business done in the ladies' hall

They just did finish the jitterbug race she
When the hooligan lash poor Claire in the face
And Claire she run with a hell of a bawl
To find the A.D.C. out in the hall

The Colonel he want to cool hooligans down
They does call him ( Two Gun Man) down in the town
But if it is order he want to restore
He better to stay at his own front door

The matter report to Jumby that night
For him to decide if right is might
With hiccoughs he said what should come to pass
She husband should kick she right in the arse

So it left for the Acting to settle next day
And two hundred bucks the hooligan pay
AND den write a letter of apology strong
And try to atone for the terrible wrong.
```

Colonel Angus Muller, C.M.G. C. St. J, was Inspector General of Police in Trinidad in the 1940s

 # Archie

AFTER THE "SUGAR REVUE" I met Archie at a dance at the Queen's Park Hotel and he didn't speak to me at all. I realised that he was annoyed that I had been in the "Sugar Revue" and had danced as a frog hopper, which was a very attractive costume but rather scanty and he didn't like me dancing in front of everyone in it. Anyway, he got over it, as he asked me out again and told me that he had been upset that I was in the "Sugar Revue".

I began to go out with Archie quite often and the more I saw him, the more I liked him; but I didn't let him know how I felt as I wasn't sure if he was really in love with me. Then one night, Archie asked me to go to a dance at "Aranguez House" where the Thavenots lived, and he said he would come and meet me at a quarter to nine. I got all dressed in my evening dress and was waiting for him to come to meet me, when Murray O'Neil came over and asked me to go to the dance with him. I said "no, I'm going with Mac" (everyone called Archie 'Mac' in those days). So he said "well, Mac has forgotten all about it, he is over at Harland's and is having a good time there". I was very upset and very angry that Archie had forgotten about his date with me. I felt that he didn't really like me that much, so when Murray said how much he wanted me to go with him, I said I would. Mother was very put out about it and said "You promised to go with Mac and should wait for him". I said "Mac has forgotten all about it and I refuse to stay at home and wait". So I went with Murray, although I didn't really want to go with him. Murray was very attentive, but after we had been at the dance for about an hour, I suddenly saw Archie there by himself and he came up to me and

Imperial College of Tropical Agriculture (I.C.T.A.) – administration building

Me standing in a beautiful garden in St. Augustine

Archie and Melba Mary, Arthur's wife, Hilda Edwards McDonald, and Arthur at the Dockyard (1931) in Antigua

Archie and me going to a party (1931)

said how sorry he was about what had happened and he wanted to explain it all to me. (He had gone to meet me and mother told him that I had gone to the dance with Murray). So I danced with him and while we were dancing he told me what had happened. He had been to see Professor Hardy about a job at the I.C.T.A., which would be a good job for him. Hardy had only asked him to come over at the last moment, and he didn't have any way of letting me know before going to see him, but he felt sure I would understand as it was of such importance to him and to his future. Of course I understood and then I was mad at Murray O'Neil, as I felt he had

Trinidad Yacht Club (1930s)

really played a dirty trick on Archie to get me to go with him to the dance. So I left the dance with Archie and had no idea what happened to Murray O'Neil.

I went to spend the weekend with the Gordons down the islands at Domos, and Archie came down for the Sunday. I was so glad to see him. I was in love with him, but he hadn't said anything to me, so I was rather distant with him. Anyway, we both left Domos after dinner and went back to the Yacht Club in the Gordons' launch. From the Yacht Club we went home in Archie's car and it was after that we both knew we loved each other very much. (Archie's reaction recorded in excerpt from his memoir: "Perhaps of the most significant things Thelma said was "I'll see you tomorrow". Suddenly tomorrow became a wonderful day to look forward to and all the tomorrows stretching into the future. I was 24 years old at the time and Thelma was 18. I have always considered it the most important day of my life and this belief has been proved by the test of time.")

A couple of weeks later we announced we were to be engaged. I realised that I was completely happy for the first time since I was grown up. I also realised that I had been in love with Archie for a long time, but never admitted it, even to myself. I know Archie was very happy too and from then on, we saw each other every day and grew closer and closer to each other, sharing all our hopes for the future. It was a very happy and contented time in our lives.

Archie got the job with Professor Fred Hardy at I.C.T.A. He worked with Pound and Pyke, and he liked his job. His job was as a research chemist in cocoa

After Archie's family reunion in Antigua 1931, his family on government launch waving goodbye to him when he was leaving Antigua for Trinidad in 1931.

research under Professor Hardy, and lecturer in physics and meteorology.

Archie had bought a secondhand car (P 4142) and it gave him very good service. We both loved the old car and our many excursions in it to places like Balandra. Monica usually came with us when we went out for the day. I think it must have been very boring for Monnie, but Archie and I never made her feel left out.

We got engaged around Christmas time, and got married about a year and a half later on July 9th, 1932. While we were engaged, Archie went to Antigua for a month to stay with his family. Arthur, Archie's brother, and his wife Mary were out for a holiday and so were Archie's two sisters, Stella and Melba, so Archie went to meet them and have a real family reunion. I missed Archie but got lots of letters from him as well.

It was lovely when Archie came back from Antigua. I was so happy and know he was glad to be back with me as well. He then had to go on a soil survey to Grenada with Professor Hardy and was away for two weeks. While he was away, I did a lot of soil maps for him (which are still in the family's possession) and I found it very interesting. I was still working at the College and doing the maps in the afternoons.

Our engagement was a very happy time and Archie and I saw a lot of each other. I worked at the College with Charlie Watts as a telephone operator (it was my first job after finishing school) and I also did the books for the staff that worked at the Sugar Refinery on the College grounds. I had to get the books to balance and use small envelopes, write the person's name on them and the amount they got. The payments were made every Friday afternoon. I also had to give first aid to any of the workers who got hurt while they were working.

Archie at I.C.T.A. Sugar Tech. Dept 1926

In the office with me were Elsie Allen and Eywoll McIntosh. I liked both of them very much and we all got on well together. Charlie Watts wasn't in the office for long periods. In the mornings, he would come in, check on letters that had come in and attended to any complaints that had been written to him from the College staff. He then left and sometimes came back after lunch. There was also a Mr. Flook who worked under Charlie Watts. I didn't like Charlie Watts, he was always telling obnoxious jokes that none of us appreciated, but he had got me the job at the College and I was grateful to him for that.

Charlie Watts lived in a nice big College house near to the small sugar factory close to our office, in fact, we were in the same grounds. His was married and his wife was very delicate. They had a little girl called Frances.

One day, there was a very bad thunder and lightning storm, and while I was sitting in front of the telephone switchboard, there was a terrific flash of lightning with the thunder following right on top it. The lightning hit the telephone board, and the flash was so close and the thunder so loud that I was stunned. Elsie and Eywoll were under their desks in the other room and shouted out to me and asked if I was alright. I said I was, but was a bit shaken up. All the telephones were out as the lightning had hit the switchboard. Neither Charlie Watts nor Mr. Flook were in the office at the time.

Sitting on a rock in the middle of Maracas river (1931)

After work, Archie often passed to pick me up and we went home together and he stayed and had tea with us. Often, we went to play tennis at the St. Augustine Club. Sometimes I went with him, but usually after coming home from work, I liked to relax and read or just do anything I wanted.

Archie usually came over after dinner and we sat in the gallery and made plans for our future. It was lovely seeing him every day, and we were very close as we shared all our dreams and hopes for the future. Mother and daddy were very understanding about leaving us alone and Monica was either in Port of Spain at school or out with her friends.

Archie lived with Dr. Mason and Dr. Macguire near the cotton station, but after he got engaged to me, he decided he didn't like living there anymore and went to board at "Hill View", the Green's guesthouse. When he would leave me at night I used to stay in the gallery, and when he got to Hill View he used to flash his torch through the window and I could see it from our house, as there was a vacant piece of land between our house and the back of Hill View. Once I knew that Archie was safely home, I would go to bed.

One time when Archie was going home to Hill View, he had a small accident. Coming out of the road from the College, he ran into a truck carrying a lot of vendors going to the market with all their goods. He said no one was hurt, as he was going very slowly and so was the truck. But he said "you have never seen such a mess, oranges, vegetables, fowls strewn all over the road and everyone talking and shouting!" Archie wasn't hurt and the car wasn't damaged, but I expect the vendors lost a lot of their produce. It was after that accident (that I hadn't known about until Archie told me the next afternoon) that I asked Archie to flash his torch and let me know that he was at home safely.

Odette Seheult got married while I was engaged to Archie and I was a bridesmaid. I wore a pink net dress with frills down to my ankles and a wide sash of pink satin and pink shoes and pink rosebuds in my hair and holding a bouquet of pink rosebuds—sounds like a lot of pink! All the bridesmaids wore the same sort of dresses, but we all wore different colours. Odette married a man called André Llanos and it was a gay wedding. Yves, Odette's brother, gave Odette away. I don't think Aunt Rosemay really liked André very much, but Odette was set on marrying him. They were happy together, but André drank too much and this was a source of worry to Odette.

After Archie and I were married, Odette was expecting a baby and got septicemia. She got very ill and wasn't expected to live. She had the baby when it was only six months and only weighed 1-1/2 pounds. It was a girl and they wrapped her in cotton wool and fed her every half hour using a dropper filled with a few drops of brandy and some special milk. No one expected the baby to live. Odette was still very ill and Aunt Rosemay stayed with her all the time. Dr. Campbell (her doctor) advised an injection of mercurochrome and eventually she began to get better. The baby also survived and when she was three months old, although still very tiny, the doctor felt her had a good chance of living. They called the baby Janice and when Janice grew up, she was very friendly with our eldest daughter Heather. Janice eventually got married to her cousin Llanos, they were not very happily married and I don't think Janice was at all happy. Odette died of cancer of the lungs while she was still quite a young woman. Poor Aunt Rosemay and Odette's husband André were in a terrible state, and André didn't live too long after she died. So Janice was left very much to the mercy of her husband. Aunt Rosemay was very close to Janice and helped her as much as she could, but she was getting old herself, so couldn't do much. After we left Trinidad I never got any news of Janice, and hope that her children grew up to be kind to her.

When Archie left the College, he got a job right away with the Department of Agriculture as Chief Inspector under the Plant Production Ordinance. He had to have a car as he travelled a lot all over the country, visiting different estates looking for plant diseases. So Archie bought a secondhand car. It was quite new and hadn't done much mileage but it had been in an accident, and the owner demanded a new car. So the money from the insurance company paid to have the car repaired properly and Archie bought it. He paid $50.00 down and I think $50.00 a month until it was paid off. It was a Morris Cowley with a canvas roof and a windscreen that could wind up. The license plate number was 4142 and it became very much part of our lives. We went everywhere in it, to the pictures, and for long drives all over Trinidad and of course, Archie used it every day to go to work and to come to see me. We had it after our marriage and I always thought of it with great affection. Of all the cars we ever had (and we had many) 4142 is always the one I will never forget.

With friends in Balandra (1932)

Our Wedding

Wedding party
Sheila Farfan, Josine Harragin, Archie, Thelma, Dr. MacGuire, Monica Seheult,
Eliane de Gannes and Betty Hardy

So time passed very happily, and we began to prepare for our wedding. We decided to get married on the 9th July, and so I began to think about my trousseau and my wedding dress etc. Our bridesmaids were Monica, my sister, Josine Harragin, Sheila Farfan and Eliane de Gannes. My wedding dress was given to me by my Aunt Anna. It was made by Miss Edwards, of white satin and tulle over a faint pink lining. The veil was of tulle with clusters of orange blossom at the side. My shoes were white Moire fabric with very fine, flesh-colour stockings. Excitement reigned supreme when I put on my wedding dress and I

Mr. and Mrs. Archie McDonald

wasn't half as nervous as I expected to be. It was quite pretty, but I often thought if I had to choose again I would have chosen a different style. The bridesmaids wore peach-coloured satin, with gold shoes and peach-coloured rosebuds, and a sort of Dutch bonnet made of peach-coloured net, they all looked very pretty.

The week before our wedding day it poured with rain every day. My poor mother and father were very worried. They had planned to have tables and chairs out on the lawn for the guests to sit as the house wasn't big enough to hold all the guests. Thank goodness the rain held up the day before and our wedding day was a lovely sunny day.

Inez Gransaull made my wedding cake (which was delicious) and Daisy Reid and Mrs. Whitehead iced it. Because of the wet weather Mrs. Whitehead and Daisy were worried that the icing wouldn't set. Anyway it all turned out well and the cake looked very nice and tasted even better.

Our wedding week went off well. Archie had asked me not to be late in coming to the church, as he was very nervous. He had already rented a house for

My wedding day, July 9th, 1932

both us to live in after we got married. It was at the end of Carmody Road and Pasea Road in St. Augustine. The house belonged to an elderly lady called Bessie Robinson and she rented it to Archie for $25.00 a month fully furnished.

Archie had already moved into the house on the 1st of July. I hired a cook, a maid called Rosie and a yard boy called Eric. So on the day we got married, Archie was already living in that house and on the way to the church he had to pass our house. As he passed with his best man, Dr. Macguire, he blew the car horn loudly to let me know that he was on his way to the church, so not to keep him waiting too long.

After about ten minutes (daddy and I were alone in the house as everyone had already left for the church), daddy said 'Well, Thellie, let's go". So off we went in daddy's car. I was sad that it was not Carrington driving us, but Carrington had been very ill and wasn't well enough to be at my wedding. I was sad about that as Carrington was like my close family.

When daddy and I got to the bottom of St. Joseph's hill, Uncle Bertie Harragin stopped us and said that Archie had not arrived at the church yet, so not to come. I found this strange as Archie had passed our house and had blown the horn to let us know that he had left. Daddy said "Thellie, are you put out?" I said I can't imagine why Archie wasn't there and then Uncle Bertie returned to say that Archie had arrived. It happened that Archie had been there all along, he had been in the vestry with Dr. Macguire and the priest. Father McDonald had got talking about Ireland where they both came from. Archie said he was getting very worried and felt he should be in the church and had tried to hurry them up.

I don't remember much about the wedding ceremony. I remember walking up the aisle with daddy and seeing Archie and Dr. Macguire waiting at the altar rails and was conscious of a sea of faces of all our friends and family. We got lots of lovely wedding presents, many of which I still have and some of which we have given to the children at different times. I remember being very happy and everyone seemed to be having a good time. I remember dancing with Archie and then Littie Hutton coming up and saying "Now I am going to dance with the bride".

When we were leaving on our honeymoon, I flung my bouquet and it was caught by Elsa Boos. I felt quite sad to part with it but remembered that flowers soon fade and by next morning my bouquet would not be the pretty thing it was on the day of my wedding.

Our Honeymoon

Archie standing next to P 4142 (1932)

At about 6:30 pm Archie and I left for our honeymoon, which we were going to spend in Balandra. Uncle Frank Maingot (he had married my father's sister Eugenie, called Jenny) had an estate house at Balandra, perched on top a hill overlooking the sea, which he lent to us. Rosie and a chauffeur called McDonald had driven there in our car 4142 with groceries, linen, clothes etc. They drove up in the morning of our wedding and Rosie settled up the house, unpacked the groceries and got everything ready for us and waited there for us to arrive. McDonald, the chauffeur, after he had left our car 4142 at the house, took a bus and came back.

Professor Fred Hardy lent us his car and Mohammed, his chauffeur, drove us to Balandra after the wedding. Besides being Fred's chauffeur, Mohammed worked at the lab at the College and often went out with Archie when he was taking soil samples. He was a very nice man. He was a Muslim and was not supposed to drink, however, he became a terrible alcoholic and eventually Fred had to get rid of him. We were all very sad about this as we all liked Mohammed very much.

We had gone up to Balandra for a week, but we were enjoying it so much that we sent a message to tell mother and daddy that we would be staying two weeks. We had lovely weather the whole time we were there and used to go out adventuring in the car nearly every day to Toco, Shark River and other places. We used to get up early in the morning and go for a swim at Balandra beach, which was very near to where we were. One morning we saw the sun rising and it was so beautiful.

On our honeymoon with our first car P 4142 (1932)

The first Sunday we were there, a lot of our friends came up for the day. It was most enjoyable and they all had a good time and left very late in the afternoon. I can't even remember what we had to eat, but I expect we had quite enough, and they all probably brought their own food. There were Ena and Johnny Agostini, Eliane de Gannes, Stanley Evelyn (he must have been in Trinidad at the time), Sheila Farfan and a doctor friend (I can't remember his name) who was working at the I.C.T.A. and wasn't a medical doctor. He was at our wedding and was a very nice young man.

One thing I remember about our honeymoon was that when we went to eat dinner, there were no knives, forks, or spoons, and when we asked Rosie about this, she said that when she unpacked the things she didn't see any. So we had one kitchen knife and fork and one kitchen spoon. Archie and I cut up our food up and ate our food the best we could with the utensils we had.

The next day we went over to Gratton and Mildred Bushe, who owned an estate in Balandra and lived quite near to where we were staying, however, there was no one there, as they had gone to Port of Spain for the weekend and to attend our wedding. Anyway, we managed without cutlery and when they came back, we borrowed some from them. We saw a lot of them and we went over to their house or they came to ours. They were glad to have someone near to them, as they were very lonely. They were a nice couple and I felt sad for them as their little son drowned when they were staying down the islands. He fell off the jetty and no one saw him and he was too young to be able to swim. It was a grief that they never got over, and Gratton said he would never have any more children. This was a stupid decision (I think) to make, as in their older years they regretted that decision very much.

On one of our excursions, we decided to go as far as the Toco Road went, so we drove a long way, all very interesting, through Toco Village on to Sans Souci and then on to Shark river where the road ended. We took many pictures of each other standing near the river which seemed to me to be quite big.

On another excursion, we passed "Aragua House" which was the Manager's house for Gordon Grant estates in Toco. Patrick Maingot was manager (he was a brother of Frank Maingot who lent us his house in Balandra). Archie said "Let's go in and see Pat Maingot, he must get lonely way up here". So we drove into the yard and called on Pat, who came out and asked us in. Mr. Harry Hutton, who was in charge of Gordon Grant estates, was staying with him for a few days and inspecting the Toco estates, so we all chatted for a bit and Harry Hutton said "What about a game of bridge?" So we stayed and played a few rubbers of bridge with them and then went back home to our house in Balandra. We got home late and Rosie said she was beginning to feel worried and a bit frightened being there by herself. Poor Rosie, she must have felt very lonely as Archie and I were out a lot and very engrossed with each other.

Our honeymoon – sunrise at Balandra.

Bessie's House, Our First Home

Bessie's House on Carmody Road, where Ian was born

AFTER TWO VERY HAPPY WEEKS in Balandra we went back to St. Augustine and to our own home, Bessie's House. It was lovely being in our own house, although I can't say I was a very good housekeeper. I had been told that I must lock up everything or the servants would rob me, so I had this big bunch of keys and kept everything locked up very securely. The trouble was I kept losing the keys and twice I went into Port of Spain and forgot to give Rosie anything to cook for lunch. However, we were fortunate that we lived very near to mother and daddy on the same road (Carmody Road), so on these occasions we descended on them and asked if they could give us some lunch and of course we got a very nice lunch. It was so nice living near to my parents and I saw them most days.

So our married life began and we were very happy. We had Rosie who cooked (I never liked cooking), made up the beds and swept out the house, and Eric who swept the yard, cut the grass, washed the car and polished the floors. I also did polishing etc. We paid Rosie $6.00 per month and all her meals. Eric was paid $5.00 per month and we gave him tea in the mornings. Bubbles, my dog, always came to our house and spent most of the day with me, but at night we made sure he went back to mother's as there were so many barking mongrels in our neighbourhood that Bubbles barked all night and kept us awake. As it was, we were often kept awake anyway by all the barking and howling dogs, this was the one snag to Bessie's House.

The house was very high from the ground and we had to walk up a long flight of stairs to get inside. There was a small front gallery, a living room, a small dining room and then a pantry and kitchen. On the east side of the house was our bedroom, a middle room, which Archie and I used as a dressing room, and a very nice room facing the road. It was an airy room with windows all around it and this we used as a sitting room and spent most of our time there. It was nice and cosy. We had our bridge table there, which we got as a wedding present and when our friends came over, this is where we sat around and played bridge.

Calypso Song Entitled
MIN-TIP "T" SHOP
Composed by Caresser

―――o―――

Chorus

At night when you are roaming
And you feel hunger is coming (repeat)
All you got to do is get up on your feet
And take a walk to 70 George Street
When you swing the corner please stop
And "Go Fah It" in at Min-Tip "T" Shop.

1st Verse

You can enjoy any privilege
If you want a beef or a ham sandwich
If egg or tin soup is your wish
Or perhaps a nice slice of fried fish
And if you want an ovaltine or so
Or call for tea, coffee or cocoa
You'll be surprised when the hunger flop
Just "Go Fah It" in at Min-Tip "T" Shop.

2nd Verse

His Motto is sanitation
And his by-word is satisfaction
With attendance able and willing
To give service for every shilling
You may be rich, poor, white or black
If you try them once "well" you must go back
So when you're hungry don't wait to drop
You could get a cheap meal at Min-Tip "T" Shop.

3rd Verse

So be wise in spending your money.
These are the days you ought to be thrifty
Min-Tip Tono makes you feel peppy
And the Milo make you feel healthy
The female attendant with her smile so sweet.
Will give you appetite when you start to eat
Don't go where they treat you abrupt
Always "Go Fah It" in at Min-Tip "T" Shop.

Caribbee Printerie. 46 Henry Street

 # Pregnancy

*A*BOUT FIVE WEEKS AFTER OUR WEDDING I began to feel ill and in the mornings. I couldn't keep down my breakfast. I thought I was having a bilious attack!! So I went over to mother's and said I was very nauseated and I would take a dose of castor oil, ugh! Mother said "Thelma, are you sure that it's a bilious attack? Perhaps you are going to have a baby." I laughed at that and said "I've only been married five weeks; I can't be expecting a baby so soon."

Mother didn't say anything more and I took the castor oil and it did no good at all and Archie didn't know what to do to help. All I could do was lie in bed and drink a little tea. By then I realised that I was pregnant and the doctor (Dr. Gibbon) came over to see me. He said I would probably feel sick for a couple of months, but would give me something to make me feel better, He made out a long prescription and that night, as I was feeling so badly, Archie gave me some of it. No sooner had I taken it that I got a very bad pain in my stomach. Well, Archie took the bottle of medicine and threw it out the window and I'm afraid I continued to feel very nauseated for the next three months.

It must have been a very trying time for Archie and he was very patient and kind and loving during all that time. I would go to see mother and she often came over to see me and consoled me and said I would soon feel better. And true enough, after three months I was feeling much better and then I was always hungry and began to feel very well. Archie was so relieved, as was I. Now I began to think of baby clothes and maternity clothes for myself, as my own clothes were becoming too tight for me around the waist.

It was about this time I remember Rosie had bought a young fowl for us to have on Sunday and she put it in a cage under the house and I went down the next day and saw the poor fowl and decided we couldn't possibly kill it, so told Rosie to cook something else for lunch, some lamb chops or salt fish pie. The day after I went to feed the fowl with some corn and found it had laid an egg. So I made a nest for it, put the egg in it and let the fowl out of the cage. After that she laid many more eggs, sat on them and eventually nine chicks hatched out. I was so thrilled and they grew well, however, mongoose took two of the chickens. I was so mad, as by this time, I had grown very attached to the little hen which was a brown speckled fowl.

And so life continued and was very happy in Bessie's House. I was now feeling very well and full of energy. Aunt Anna and mother made all the baby clothes and I only had to make a few things.

I remember one day I had to go into Port of Spain with mother to spend the day with grandma, Aunt Anna and Aunt Muriel. They were all so happy that I was going to have a baby and that grandma was going to be a great-great-grandmother and Aunt Anna a great-great-aunt.

While I was there (they still lived in Cipriani Boulevard which brought back so many memories of my school days) Archie rang to say that he had heard that the Building & Loan were giving out share certificates and he would really be glad if we could get some, so would I go down to the Building & Loan and get as many as I could. I rang daddy at the Public Works and asked if Carrington could bring me to the Building & Loan and daddy said he would send Carrington right away. (Carrington was now better from his illness and we were all so happy to have him back with us).

So I went to the B & L and got as many application forms as I could and got mother, grandma, Aunt Anna, Aunt Muriel to all apply for shares and I sent in applications for Archie and me. Every application form allowed you three shares. The idea was if mother etc. got any shares, they would give them to us. Funnily enough, Archie and I were the only ones who got shares. We were very lucky, so we started a savings scheme with the B & L, which was a good company. We paid $6.00 a month. Archie and I were thrilled, and we kept a strict budget—rent, servants, food and pocket money and what was left over we saved. We had no electric light, so didn't have that to pay, and we only paid for water annually and that was a very small amount. Now, of course we had to save up for the expenses of the baby's arrival, doctor's fee, nurses fees etc. Mother said "why don't you get Nurse Dottin, she has always been with the family and I had her for Monica." I was very pleased to have Nurse Dottin, but looking back I realise that she really knew very little about babies, and as I was very ignorant about babies and had no friends who had babies, and mother remembered very little, I am sorry I didn't have a more knowing midwife as it would have saved me a lot of worry and anxiety.

Many friends came to see us when we lived at Bessie's, amongst them was Tonia and Cory Davies. It was the first time that I had met them and liked them very much. They were to turn out to be amongst the best friends we had, if not the best. When they first came to see us, Tonia could speak very little English. She was Spanish, and Cory had met her when he worked in Cuba. They had two little boys, Cory (jr) and Frank. Cory was about 3 years old and Frank about one. Archie often went to the St. Augustine Club to play tennis and have a game of bridge with his friends and I would go down to mother's and daddy's and sometimes Monica came over to see me.

The guard house at Government House.

Birth of our First Baby

THE TIME WAS GETTING NEAR for the baby to arrive and I started to get very excited. I remember it was Easter Monday and Vera Johnson and Edith Trestrail (two sisters who lived in St. Augustine and whom we knew well) had come to see us and we were all sitting in the little sitting room talking. No sooner had they gone than I began having slight pains, particularly in my back, and realised that the baby would soon be coming. I told Archie and both he and I were very excited, although I think Archie was a bit worried and nervous. When I was sure that the baby would soon be coming, Archie went down the road to mother and daddy and told them. Daddy sent Carrington into Port of Spain to get Nurse Dottin and mother and Monica came to be with me, and Archie went to tell Dr. Gibbon. Dr. Gibbon calmly told Archie as it was a first baby, it was sure to be a while before he was needed but he would come to see me.

Nurse Dottin arrived and got a nice hot bath ready for me while she 'prepared' me for the baby's delivery. The pains were still not very severe and I thought to myself 'this is not so much to make a fuss about, I wonder why everyone says it is so bad,' however, I was soon to find out otherwise. All night I had pains, although they were not severe. Dr. Gibbon would come and check and then leave again, saying everything was normal and that the pains weren't bad yet! So he would come back when he thought it was time.

Monica and mother went home to get some sleep, daddy came up and kissed me and left, I know he was feeling very apprehensive, Archie went into the living to get some sleep, but as he was coming in to see me constantly, I doubt he got much sleep. All this was on Easter Monday. On Tuesday morning the pains began to get worse and Dr. Gibbon came and stayed with me most of the day. By now the pains were bad and I wondered how much longer this would go on. Poor Archie was in a state by this time and I was sorry that I hadn't told him to go to the office. He couldn't do anything for me and just sitting and waiting must have been intolerable for him.

Eventually our baby was born at six o'clock on Tuesday afternoon. He was a lovely big, strong baby boy, weighing 9-3/4 lbs. Archie was so relieved and so proud of his son and so was I. In fact so was the whole family. I had to have a few stitches which were rather painful but I was so glad that our baby was born and he was alright.

Someone had lent me a bassinet which Aunt Anna had done up beautifully for me and we put Ian (our baby son) in it. I slept very little that night, I was uncomfortable and excited and kept listening for the baby. Archie had said, "if the baby is a boy, I would like it to be called Ian." So from the moment he was born we called him Ian. Of course mother, Monica and I think daddy were there when Ian was born and everyone was happy and relieved.

After Ian was born I felt very weak and had no appetite and I'm sure the doctor should have given me a tonic, but he didn't, so I didn't feel as well as I should have and I also worried a lot. Anyway, all that soon passed and I began to enjoy my baby and Archie continued to be a great joy and support to me.

I was a very worried young mother. I felt I knew nothing about babies and everything worried me. Nurse Dottin wasn't much help as I think she herself was unsure. Thank goodness I had a very sensible husband who said "Thellie, stop worrying, you have a strong healthy baby and there is nothing to worry about." Nurse Dottin left after a month, and when she left I was even more worried. Anyway, Rosie found a very nice person to look after the baby. She was a big strong young woman called Vio who turned out to be a real treasure. She not only looked after the baby, but she looked after me as well *(note 9)*.

When Ian was about one month old, Fanny Whitehead came to see us and said that her husband was resigning from his job and they wanted to go to England for a year and see how they liked living there, so they wanted someone to rent their house during that period and wondered if we would be interested in taking it. She would rent it to us for the same rent we were paying Bessie for renting her house. Archie and I talked it over and decided to take it, it was a nice house with large grounds and lots of fruit trees and it would be much quieter than Bessie's. However, no sooner had we decided this and told Mrs. Whitehead that we would take the house, Mrs. Whitehead got very ill and died quite soon after.

I can't remember the details of what happened to the house between the time that Mrs. Whitehead died and we moved in, all I remember was that I went up to the house while Archie was in England and I was staying with mother and met Mrs. Waddell (Mrs. Whitehead's sister) at Fanny Whitehead's house to make arrangements for when Archie and I would move in. Mrs. Waddell told me that Mrs. Whitehead had left a lot of her furniture to different members of her family and they had all taken what was theirs. Anyway they left us the basic things. I didn't see Mr. Whitehead at all, I suppose that after Fanny's death he had gone to England.

Boat Trip to Antigua

When Ian was three months old, Archie got long leave from the College, so we all went up to Antigua to stay with Archie's parents. I brought Vio with us as she was such a good nurse to Ian and such a help to me. I was very fond of Vio and so was Archie. Nothing was too much for her to do for us. Rosie left when we left and so did Eric the yard boy, both had been devoted help to us. Rosie got another job and so did Eric. I am sure that Eric did well as he was a good worker and a nice person and he was ambitious to get on.

Before we went to Antigua, I had a lot of new dresses made. Gussie Garcia who lived in St. Joseph and whom I knew from the time I had lived in St. Joseph, made them for me. Gussie was a very good dressmaker and she was young and had good taste, so the dresses she made for me were very pretty and I really looked nice in them. Gussie Garcia was a cousin of Malia Gonzalez whom I knew well from school in St. Joseph and they lived next door to each other. Gussie was the only girl in a family of about six boys. She was a nice person and was engaged to a nice young man called Edgar Ford who worked at Bonanza Store in Port of Spain.

Mother, daddy, Monica and of course Bubbles moved to Port of Spain at the same time as we were leaving for Antigua. I knew that when we came back that we wouldn't be so near to them, and it made me a bit sad as I loved them all very much and loved being able to go to see them most days, or they would come over to see me. So while we were in Antigua they moved to a house in Belmont. It was a nice house that was quite near to the Savannah.

R.M.S. "Lady Rodney"

Archie, I, Ian and Vio left on a "Lady Boat" for Antigua. I am not sure which one it was. There were three Lady Boats that made their way from Canada all through the islands as far as Trinidad, *Lady Hawkins, Lady Rodney* and *Lady Nelson* (*note 10*).

We left Trinidad at about 10 o'clock at night and mother, daddy and Monica had dinner with us on board before the boat left. We had a lovely trip up the islands. We had a nice cabin and Vio had a cabin next to us. She was a real godsend to Archie and me. Vio looked after Ian so well, Archie and I felt completely free to enjoy the whole voyage.

Grenada was our first stop. We arrived about 7 o'clock the following morning and had time to go ashore and have a swim at Grande Anse Beach. We were at ease doing this as Vio was looking after Ian. The Lady Boat left Grenada at 11 o'clock and we arrived in St. Vincent at about 3 pm. We went ashore to see Lorna and Andréw Bryant (Lorna was Josine's Harragin's sister and she had married a post graduate student from I.C.T.A. and he now had a job in St. Vincent. They had a little girl about a year old called Mary Anne. We stayed and had tea and chatted about Trinidad and the College, and I gave Lorna news of all her family in Trinidad. At 4:30 pm, Stanley Evelyn arrived to take Archie and me around St. Vincent. It was very good of him, but it was getting late and we seemed to be in a very remote part of the island, and I began to get worried that we wouldn't be able to get back in time to board the Lady Boat before it left the island at 10 o'clock that night. I imagined all sorts of things, like the car breaking down or getting a puncture, and wondered what Vio would do if we didn't make it back in time. Of course, most of all I worried about my baby who was only 3 months old and I was still breast feeding him, although I had left a bottle of milk for him and Vio knew how to prepare it. Well, we did get back in time, and I was so happy to be back with Ian that I resolved I would never take that risk again. Stanley had dinner with us on board before the boat left at 10 p.m.

The next morning we docked in Barbados and stayed there for two days, which was really nice. The first day we went ashore and had a swim at Engineer's Pier and returned to the boat for lunch. That night we went with a lot of other passengers to a dance at Engineer's Pier. I wore one of the dresses that Gussie had made for me, it was very pretty and I got a lot of compliments. It was nice to feel slim and pretty again, after being pregnant and big and uncomfortable. And what a boon it was to Archie and me to have Vio with us, whom we could depend on to look after Ian while we were out enjoying ourselves.

The next day we stayed on board the boat and asked Vio if she would like to go ashore and see Barbados, but she said she didn't know anyone on the island and would rather stay with us and Ian. We spent most of the day on deck, reading and relaxing with Ian in a pram next to us. I was still a little worried about Ian and was always apprehensive that something may happen to him—I was so ignorant when it came to young babies.

The following day we left for St. Lucia and went ashore in the afternoon to have tea with Eddie Baynes and his wife at Government House. Eddie Baynes was the governor of St. Lucia (he was a cousin of Archie's mother). Government House was in a lovely high spot overlooking the harbour, and we had a good view of the Lady Boat. We enjoyed the tea and liked Eddie and his wife. At 6 o'clock the flag was pulled down and we all stood at attention while it was brought down. After that we were driven back to the boat in the governor's car!

After St. Lucia we sailed for Dominica and we just saw it from the Lady Boat, we didn't go ashore, and then set sail for Montserrat. The sea between Dominica and Montserrat was very rough and for the first time I felt seasick, which was most inconvenient as Antigua was our next stop and we had to finish all the last minute packing. So I was very thankful Archie was helping me, while Vio looked after Ian.

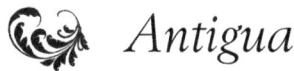 # Antigua

As we approached Antigua I began to feel a bit nervous about meeting Archie's parents and all his relations and friends. However, from the letters I had received from Archie's mother and father, I knew they were nice people and were looking forward to meeting me and very excited to see their grandson.

The Lady Boat docked far outside the harbour and we had to take a launch to the jetty in St. John's. Archie's mother and father were waiting for us on the dock and they were so nice and kind to me and so delighted with their grandson that I soon stopped being nervous and began to relax and enjoy myself. Archie's parents lived in a big wooden house on Redcliffe Street in St. John's, it was called "Redcliffe House". I liked it very much. I particularly liked the big living room which was always cool and shady as there was a big stone verandah facing the street with green trellis work, and on the east side was a big a stone gallery with lots of ferns and plants.

There was also a garden with a huge sandbox tree at the far end, which made it a lovely shady garden. The bedrooms were upstairs and Archie, Ian and I had the north bedroom that faced the road, but in those days there was very little traffic so it wasn't very noisy. However, there was a street light which shone into our room and that bothered me a bit as I liked to sleep in a very dark room at night time.

All Archie's relatives came over to see us as well as lots of Dr. and Mrs. McDonald's friends. We were asked out a lot, so it was a good thing we had Vio!

Dr. William M. McDonald and Hilda McDonald née Edwards, Archie's parents. St Kitts (1905)

The Bungalow - Gray's Hill, St. Johns Antigua - Home of Hon. and Mrs. Donald McDonald, parents of Ian Donald Roy McDonald (note 12).

I remember going to see Archie's grandmother, Granny Edwards, and taking Ian to see her. She was thrilled with her great-grandson. Granny Edwards was an invalid and lived in Church Lane. Her son, Uncle Reggie Edwards, Archie's mother's brother, had bought the house for her. She had to have someone living with her as she was unable to look after herself. Archie's mother also went to see her every day.

We also went to see Aunt Maggie McDonald, who was Dr. McDonald's eldest sister and Archie's godmother. She lived in St. John's street at the "Bungalow". Aunt Maggie was blind and could do very little for herself; a Miss Moore lived with her and looked after her and her home. I loved Aunt Maggie and was disappointed that she couldn't see our little son. It was also the last time that I saw her, as on subsequent visits she was no longer alive.

Then there was Aunt Gyppie and Uncle Clydie McDonald. Uncle Clydie was Dr. McDonald's brother, I think he was the youngest in the family. They lived at "High Point House" on High Point Estate, which Uncle Clydie owned. They had two children, Roy and Jean.

High Point was a lovely old house with Demerara windows and green trellises. When I was staying at Redcliffe House, one of the things that surprised me was Dr. McDonald ringing up Uncle Clydie every night and saying, "Clydie, did you have

Dr William M McDonald, Archie's father

rain today?" And if Clydie said yes, then Dr. McDonald (grandpa) would ask "how many parts?" Of course, this was very important to Uncle Clydie as High Point Estate was in a very dry area and as Uncle Clydie grew sugar cane to send to the Antigua Sugar Factory, a good rainfall made all the difference to him. Coming from Trinidad, where we had definite rainy seasons and dry seasons, it seemed odd to me.

Uncle Clydie and Aunt Gyppie often came to Redcliffe House and brought Roy and Jean, who were small children, with them. They were a great joy in Uncle Clydie and Aunt Gyppie's life. We also often went to High Point House to see them. It was a really old-fashioned, large wooden house, with a stone gallery and stone kitchen, and a big wide staircase going upstairs to the bedrooms. It was on a point overlooking the sea and there was always a strong wind blowing. Often, Uncle Clydie and Aunt Gyppie did not open the big windows as we would have been blown away! After 6 o'clock the mosquitoes were very bad and everyone was slapping and brushing them away. Often visitors put their legs into pillow cases to keep from being badly bitten. I don't think they were malaria mosquitoes, just big bush mosquitoes.

I really liked Aunt Gyppie and Uncle Clydie. Uncle Clydie was blind and Aunt Gyppie was deaf, and Uncle Clydie often said "Gyppie is my eyes and I am her ears." They were a dear, dear couple and got on so well together. In later years, every time Archie and I and the children went to Antigua we always saw a lot of them. Their son Roy eventually went to school in England and then straight from school into World War II. I think he was mostly in North Africa with the Tank Division. Roy stayed in England after the war and became a mining engineer and did very well. Roy married a girl called Barbara from Cornwall and at the time of writing this memoir, they were still happily married. They have two or three girls all of whom I think are married. They had a baby while Roy was working at the Antigua Sugar Factory.

Jean, their daughter, married an American from the base in Antigua during the war. I think his name was Peterson. They had no children as Jean couldn't have any, so they adopted three children—first a boy, then a girl (who turned out to be very ungrateful, left home, and they never heard of her again), and after many years, another little girl who was, I think, a great joy to them.

Hilda Edwards McDonald, Archie's mother

To be near to Uncle Clydie and Aunt Gyppie, Roy took a job at the Antigua Sugar Factory. Unfortunately, the job at the factory didn't work out as Roy found that there was no future in it, so he left and they went back to England. This made Uncle Clydie and Aunt Gyppie sad, as Jean and her husband had gone to live in the States, leaving Uncle Clydie and Aunt Gyppie very much alone in their old age.

Uncle Clydie and Aunt Gyppie had so little in their lives as far as money was concerned. High Point Sugar Estate was a poor one and when World War II started, the estate was taken away from him for an American base to be built there. The sum of money they gave him was small even for those days, so you can imagine what it would be in these days. After the war, all the land was given back to the Antigua government. We (Archie's family) felt very strongly that it

High Point, Antigua (1930s), home of Archie's Uncle Clydie and Aunt Gyppie

should have been given back to Uncle Clydie and his family. Today that land is one of the choice pieces of land in Antigua and Uncle Clydie and Aunt Gyppie would have been well off.

Although Uncle Clydie and Aunt Gyppie were allowed to live at High Point House for their lifetime, after their death it went back to the Antigua government, who converted it into flats (real vandalism). Many years later, when Roy and Barbara went out to Antigua for a holiday, they tried to buy the house and restore it to its original state, but the government refused to sell it to them. Roy and Barbara now own a house in Cornwall, England called "High Point".

In those days, the Antigua Sugar Factory was the hub of life and society in Antigua. All the people who worked at the factory lived in the area around it, forming a community of its own, with nice houses. Everyone there entertained a lot and we often went to the sugar factory compound to visit friends and have dinner or tea with them—not so much on our first visit, but during our future visits. During our first visit, Mr. Henzell was the manager of the sugar factory and MacMichael was the chief engineer. Both were very good at their jobs and under their guidance the factory did very well.

I remember Mr. and Mrs. Henzell coming to visit grandma and grandpa McDonald at Redcliffe House. Mrs. Henzell was quite a character. One thing I remember very well about her was that she was never without a cigarette in her mouth. In the latter part of her life, many years after, when Archie, I and the

Archie's sisters Stella and Melba in tennis gear (l) and at Carpenter's Rock (r), 1931

children stayed at Cliff House in Antigua with grandma and grandpa (Archie's parents had moved from Redcliffe House as St. John's was getting too noisy and all their friends had moved out), Mrs. Henzell came to see us and she was smoking a cigar. She said the doctor had told her to stop smoking cigarettes, so she now smoked cigars. She eventually died of cancer of the throat.

The Henzells had five children. Their sons were Max, who did very well and lived in Jamaica; Len, who worked in the oilfields in Trinidad and married a Trinidadian girl called Mavis de Boehmler and they had four children, three girls and a boy, whom our children knew very well; and Frank, who lived in Antigua and spent the last years of his life living on Long Island (now called Jumby Bay, a real millionaire's paradise) raising sheep and living the life of a hermit. He married a very pretty English girl and they had one daughter, but they didn't get along and eventually got a divorce.

Frank didn't want any money from his parents when they died, he just asked that they would leave him Long Island in their will. I think his father thought Frank was a bit crazy to just want Long Island, as he had originally bought it for just about one hundred and twenty five pounds.

Eventually, when Frank Henzell got very ill, he sold Long Island for $1/2 million dollars, which was considered a fantastic price in those days. Long Island changed hands many times in the following years and at the writing of this memoir, is owned by the Mahani family in America, and they have made it into a beautiful place with its own desalination plant, a golf course, beautiful villas and hotel and homes. It is considered to be one the best hotels in the world!

The Henzells also had two daughters, Judy, who married Moody Stuart, and Joan who married someone from the factory called Simmons. Judy I never met but I did meet her husband, Alec Moody Stuart, who was a big shot and very wealthy. They eventually left Antigua to live in England.

(*Note*: While I was in Antigua on my first visit, Joan Simmons was also in Antigua on holiday with her little girl of about three years old. Joan was staying with her parents at the Big House at the sugar factory. She had a crush on Roger Edwards and went out of her way to flirt with him. He, however, was not at all interested and never gave her any encouragement.)

The Antigua Sugar Factory continued to be the hub of Antigua's social life for many years, and now it is sad to see it all gone to ruins and the houses run down and dilapidated, as sugar is not an industry in Antigua anymore. I miss so much seeing sugar cane growing all over Antigua with its arrows waving in the wind. This was a sight one saw anywhere one drove in Antigua. Now all this land is wasteland, with only cassie growing on it, and some of it fenced in and cattle being reared by the government. What happens to the cattle is a mystery to me, as most of the beef we got in Antigua comes from Australia or New Zealand, and we certainly never got fresh milk. Those days seem so far in the past now. Today Antigua is focused on tourism and all the young people of the old families have left and the older generations have died, so now it is a land of strangers who come and stay a year or two and then leave. No one puts down roots here anymore. Archie and I, Maybert and Dalmer Dew, Phyllis and Marjorie Branch are the only old timers left. In our old age we live a very reclusive sort of life. If we go out, it is only to St. John's to shop and go to the bank. We are very lucky to have our daughter Gillian and her husband Douglas Howie living with us. We would not have been able to continue to live here alone and would have had to sell the house and buy a little flat in England to live there. As neither Archie or I liked the cold, we wouldn't have liked living in England at all. I remember I would often tell Archie "I would like to live near the sea when I am getting old", so I got my wish, not only do I live near the sea, but the house sits right on a cliff overlooking the water (hence the name Cliff House, built by Archie's parents in 1947).

After that short interlude, I will revert back to our first visit when we stayed at Redcliffe House.

Mr. and Mrs. Forest lived next door to Archie's parents, and during our stay there, I often went over to visit Mrs. Forest who was a great friend of grandma's and she didn't keep very good health. Grandma spent a lot of time with her and grandpa attended to her. I would take Ian with me when I visited. Mr. Forest was not very interested in Ian, he was a peculiar sort of man and very taken with his fossils (he was a bit of a fossil himself I thought).

We also met the MacAndrews; Mrs. MacAndrew was grandpa's sister. And they had five daughters and the last one was a son, Douglas. We got to know Douglas very well. He married Mary Shepherd, who was the granddaughter of Dean Shepherd, a well-known and well-loved clergyman in Antigua. His wife, Mrs. Shepherd, was also a beloved Antiguan character.

Then there was Aunt Em and her two daughters Muffi and Gwenette. We saw them often and we had a lovely dinner with them which Aunt Em prepared (she was a very good cook) and Gwenette made a lovely pineapple ice box cake. Archie as a young man, just from school in England, had had a crush on Muffi, and I know she and Aunt Em must have been very disappointed that Archie hadn't married her. However, they were all very nice to me and I appreciated this very much. Aunt Em had a special place in my heart as she had looked after Archie when he was a young man during the time he had been so desperately ill (*note 12*). Archie's mother was in England at the time and couldn't get back to Antigua (there were no planes in those days) and Aunt Em had moved into Redcliffe House and nursed Archie and cooked meals for him that he was able to eat. Archie never forgot what she had done for him and I never did either.

I remember Aunt Em staying with us in Trinidad. Muffi and her husband, along with their two children and nurse, also stayed with us for over a month on their way to Jamaica. It was a trying time for us as we didn't like her husband, but I'm glad we did it for Muffi.

Then there were the Frank Goodwins at their Gaynor's Estate, where we often went for a very lavish tea on a Sunday afternoon, and afterwards we would

Me with Ruth Hutson, Joan Simmons and daughter, cousin Roger Edwards and Archie's sister Melba at Dockyard (1933)

play clock golf. It was always most enjoyable and Gaynor's always had a special place in my heart as a happy place to go to. We also went to the 'Bob' Goodwins for tea along with a lot of other Antiguans, also very enjoyable, but I preferred Gaynor's. The Bob Goodwin's had no children, which was always a sorrow for them. The Frank Goodwin's had one daughter, Doreen, and one night we went to a large dinner party that they had for Doreen who had just come out from school in England.

Then there was the younger crowd and we went to dances at Fort James, but I didn't like to go out so often as I didn't like leaving Ian. Grandma (Archie's mother, I called her grandma when the children started calling her grandma) rented a house for us at Corbison's Point, as she thought we would enjoy being by the sea. Actually both Archie and I hated it. It rained a lot and the mud around the house was very sticky and stuck to the soles of our shoes. Also, the flies were awful and so was the glare from the sea. I got quite ill with dysentery while I was there and felt very badly. Conditions were quite primitive. I was so worried about Ian getting it that I wouldn't let him come close to me. So Vio and Archie had to take complete charge of Ian. Dr. McDonald, Archie's father, came to see me and prescribed castor oil and kaolin. I got over it but still felt very badly. Why we stayed on at Corbison's Point for as long as we did I will never know.

Archie's cousin Roger Edwards had come out to Antigua for a holiday while he was at Cambridge College in the UK. His father, Reggie Edwards, who lived in South Africa, wanted his son Roger to see Antigua, so sent him out for a holiday during the summer vacation. Granny Edwards, Archie's grandmother, got to see her grandson from South Africa, which pleased her very much. Roger also stayed at Redcliffe House while we were there. Archie then went to England for about two months, and I stayed in Antigua for a short time after he left, and grandma, Melba, Roger, Ruth Hudson, myself, Ian and Vio all went to stay at

Nelson Dockyard Barracks, where we stayed with Archie's family in 1933.

the Dockyard for ten days. Aunt Em came with us and I enjoyed that, though I missed Archie very much and wished he was there with us.

While we were staying at the Dockyard a mild hurricane hit us. And even though we closed up all the doors with large wooden hurricane shutters, the rain still got in. I was worried about my baby, as it was difficult getting water and I needed to keep things sterilised with boiling water. The hurricane lasted about eight hours and then we were able to open the shutters and get water. I don't know what I would have done without Vio, who got us water and a coal pot from outside, boiled water for Ian and made us all tea, which we had with bread and butter. I really missed not having Archie with me, as he would have been a great help. I can't remember Roger helping much. I was quite glad to get back to Redcliffe House and live a routine life again, and was looking forward to going back to Trinidad to stay with mother, daddy and Monica until Archie came back home... I was already counting the days.

Archie left Antigua by the *Ingoma* or *Inanda* (*note 11*). After he left, I was very lonely without him and missed him terribly. He was such a loving, thoughtful and wise young man and as I was young, I depended on his advice and wisdom. So when he left, life seemed very empty. Archie's parents were very nice to me and I had my little son who was such a joy. Vio knew I missed my husband and was always saying "Mr. McDonald will come back soon." So the time passed and I looked forward to getting back to Trinidad as I knew after that it wouldn't be long before Archie would be back.

Return Boat Trip to Trinidad

Just before my departure from Antigua, Roger Edwards came to tell me that as I was going to Trinidad by Lady Boat, he decided to come along as well, since he would really like to see all the different islands and Trinidad in particular. I was a little apprehensive about him coming to Trinidad as I felt I would have to bring him around and introduce him to my friends, when all I really wanted to do was to be settled with mother, daddy and Monica until Archie came back from England.

I told Roger that if he wanted to go to Trinidad, of course he could, but I warned him that he couldn't stay with my parents as the house was too small, so he would have to stay in a hotel, he said he understood this.

Then the time came for us to leave. Vio helped me pack and I had to remember all the things I would need for Ian on the trip. I was sorry to say goodbye to Archie's parents who had been so good to me while I was in Antigua, but I was glad to be getting back to Trinidad and seeing my family again.

Vio slept with me in the cabin and I was so glad to have her company as I didn't have Archie with me. Vio as usual was a great help and often brought in my breakfast as I was feeling a bit seasick. Vio wasn't at all seasick. Roger kept bursting into the cabin and asking wasn't I coming down for breakfast, or wasn't I coming up on deck, or wasn't I going ashore. I told him that I had been ashore with Archie and didn't want to go ashore again. I wanted to just sit on deck and relax. I didn't realise that a lot of the other passengers thought that Roger was my

The Union Club on Marine Square in Port of Spain was a meeting place for businessmen and planters who were overnighting in Port of Spain.

husband as he was usually with me and had meals with Ian and me. I must say they must have thought we were a very indifferent young couple.

The first time I realised what the other passengers were thinking was one morning, when I was sitting on deck reading a book with Ian in his pram besides me. A young man (a New Zealander) came and sat next to me and struck up a conversation. I was annoyed about this, as I was enjoying my book and didn't want to talk to a complete stranger. Anyway, after a while he said, "Would you mind if I gave you a piece of advice?" At first, I was rather taken aback but said, "No, not at all". He then said, "Well, I think you should go ashore with your husband sometimes, you have a nurse for your baby and your husband would like you to go ashore with him sometimes". I was so astonished at what he was saying I burst out, "Do you really think Roger is my husband? Well, he isn't, my husband is in England for a short stay, and Roger is my husband's cousin and he happens to be going to Trinidad, so that is why we are often together!"

After that I was very careful of how I treated Roger, as Roger was always sitting with me. I never danced with him in the evening and told him I didn't feel inclined to dance (that meant I couldn't dance with anyone else) and encouraged him to dance with any unattached young woman who was around.

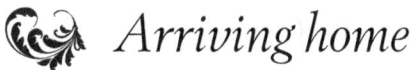 Arriving home

MOTHER AND DADDY were waiting to meet us when we arrived in Trinidad and I was so happy to see them. I introduced Roger to them, but we had no room in the car to give him a lift. He said he would take a taxi and go to the Queen's Park Hotel and try to get a cheap room.

At mother and daddy's I shared a room with Monica. It was a big room so Ian stayed in the room with us. The house only had two big bedrooms upstairs and a nice dressing room. Downstairs was a verandah and a living room, dining room, pantry and kitchen and maid's quarters. Vio was very happy to be back in Trinidad and she went home for three days. I missed her a lot, but I was lucky to have mother and Monica to help me.

Daddy had arranged with Public Works to make me a lovely baby's crib, but when it arrived we couldn't get up the stairs, so we had to get it through one of the windows in the upstairs bedroom. And what a time the men had getting on the outside roof and pulling it up with ropes and then to get it through the window! Thank goodness the windows were very large! Finally, I was safely settled in with mother and daddy and busy planning the move to Whitehead's House in St. Augustine. I knew that when Archie came back he would want to move into our own house. I missed him so much and was counting the days for him to come back. I got lots of letters from him and he sounded so homesick, and longing to get back to me and his little son.

Then there was Roger Edwards who didn't know what to do with himself so was often at the house. My father was very good to him and whenever he was going out into the country he would bring Roger with him, and in this way Roger could see some of Trinidad. Sometimes, in the afternoon, daddy lent us the car and with Carrington driving, I brought Roger to meet some of my friends. I also brought him to meet Josine, Uncle Bertie and Aunt Rosie Harragin who were nice to him and threw a small party welcoming party for him.

I also brought him to meet Betty and Toodie Fraser and we all drove up to Mount St. Benedict. I was sorry that Monica wasn't old enough to go out with Roger, but she was only fifteen and she had her own set of teenage friends. I know that mother didn't like me being out so much in Roger's company and would be very glad when he left. To tell the truth, I was very glad when he left as well, and I didn't feel that I had to show him around.

Before Archie came back, I went to dinner twice with the Murrays in St. Augustine. Girlie (Manuelita Murray) and her father came to pick me up and brought me back home. I thought it was very nice of them to do this.

I went to see Mrs. Waddell about moving into Mrs. Whitehead's house and fixed the date to move in and everything was prepared so that as soon as Archie arrived we would be able to move in. By this time I was getting very excited at the thought of Archie's return, and I knew he would see a big difference in Ian, who was now six months old and a really lovely baby, fat and chubby and strong with a lovely colour and his hair very fair and beginning to curl a little.

Vio took him to the Queen's Park Savannah every morning and afternoon and I got so many compliments about him and what a lovely, healthy baby he was. He was now sitting up and played a lot in his crib with his toys. His great delight was to throw them out of the crib and then shout so that someone would come and put them all back in again.

My big worry when I stayed with mother and daddy in Belmont were the ticks that Bubbles seemed to collect from the field behind the house and then come into the house and shed them. I found ticks crawling up the walls and I was so worried that they would get into Ian's crib. Carrington would bathe Bubbles every day and put a lot of disinfectant in the water, but as soon as he went outside he would come back covered with ticks. It was really a worry, and it was difficult keeping Bubbles out of the rooms upstairs. Poor Bubbles—it must have been most frustrating for him! And for us it was a very worrying thing.

And so time went by and Archie was due back, and I went over to Whitehead's House to get everything organised for his return. I was very excited. Daddy, mother and Monica had been so good to me while I stayed with them, but they knew I missed Archie very much.

Archie arrived early in the morning. I can't remember which day it was or which month. Aunt Muriel came with me on the launch to meet him and we went on board the boat. Both Archie and I were so happy to be together again. Carrington was waiting for us by the lighthouse jetty and we all went up to the house in Belmont to see mother and daddy and collect Ian and Vio and go up to our house in St. Augustine. Daddy had already sent up the crib and our suitcases and everything I had at Belmont, so it was Archie, Vio and Ian to go to St. Augustine with Carrington.

Downtown Port of Spain

The Whitehead's House

Whitehead's House on Circular Road, where Heather was born.

It was nice to be in our own home again and we were so happy to be together once more. Archie couldn't get over how much Ian had grown while he was away and all the things he could do.

The day after we arrived in St. Augustine, we got a new car, it was a Baby Austin, a nice little car with a sunshine roof that we could pull aside and let in the sun (needless to say we never needed this in Trinidad). However, we both missed 4142, our old Morris car, which we had used so much while we were engaged and on our honeymoon. Even when I think of it now in my old age, I think of 4142 with great affection. It is the only car that really meant a lot to me. I can't remember whether we traded it in and got the Baby Austin or if he sold it.

The Whitehead's House was a nice house, but it had no electric lights, and I used to find it rather dismal at nighttime.

We had a Petromax lamp which we lit and used in the dining room and drawing room, but the bedrooms always seemed dark and a bit depressing with shadows cast around the room by the oil lamps.

We had a big orchard with lots of julie mango trees, but not many other fruit trees. In the front of the house was a big driveway which was very nice to push Ian around in his pram. When he got old enough to walk and play around outside, it is where he spent a lot of his time. He had a lovely little ice cream cart which he liked to push around and fill up with little stones and pebbles and pretend to be selling ice creams.

I remember it was very wet for the nearly two years we spent at

Archie with Ian at Macqueripe Beach

the Whitehead's House, and the back of the house where the orchard was, was usually wet and soggy, so Ian would generally play in the front of the house which was very nice. The Whiteheads didn't have a car, so they didn't have a garage, but they had built one for us. The Whitehead House was situated on St. Augustine Circular Road, which was quite near to Carmody road where mother and daddy, Monica and I had lived for many years. It was close to the I.C.T.A. staff houses and our nearest neighbours were Bo and Duggie Patterson (I expect Duggie's real name was Douglas) who lived at the corner house just opposite to us. They were very nice people and both Archie and I liked them very much. They had two little girls, Susan and Ann, and stayed at the College for many years. When Ian was much older he was friendly with the two Patterson girls, even though they were older than he was. We also lived close to the Shepherds and the Gianettis. Mr. Corbin, who used to run the hostel for students, also lived not far from us. Mr. and Mrs. Corbin had two children, Maurice and Muriel, but they were more my age.

Archie continued working at the I.C.T.A. under Professor Fred Hardy. Fred had a very high opinion of Archie's work and his all around knowledge and ability. He often said "My, what a clever devil Archie is". He was a very good friend to Archie and always helped him in his career. I was very fond of Fred. I had some reservations about his wife Sally who was inclined to laugh at people behind their backs and make fun of them. I certainly didn't like this trait in her character. Fred and Sally had one little girl, Betty, who was my little train-bearer at our wedding and was a dear little girl but a little too fat. She looked more like Fred than Sally.

We often went to see Fred and Sally. They also lived on Circular Road, but at the opposite side to where we lived. They lived in one of the college houses which were big and spacious. Fred's hobby was his lovely vegetable garden where he worked every afternoon when he came back from the office. Fred didn't play games such as tennis or golf, so his recreation was working in his garden. Many were the times that he gave us a big bag of freshly grown vegetables, string beans, artichokes, Lima beans etc. And Archie and I enjoyed them very much.

While we were at the Whitehead's House, Archie grew some lovely tomatoes; they were the biggest and juiciest tomatoes that I have ever tasted, so sweet and not many seeds. We often tried after that to grow tomatoes again, but they were never like the first ones that Archie grew. We had so many julie mangoes, we would sell them and also give a lot of them to our friends and of course to mother, daddy, grandma and Aunt Anna. We also gave Fred and Sally as many as they wanted. There was also an Indian man who used to come with his rod and bag and pick the mangoes and he paid us a penny for one. The money we made from the mangoes helped to pay the gardener John. John was an Indian man who had been with the Whiteheads for many years and he kept the grounds tidy. I don't think his name was John but that is what Mr. Whitehead called him.

Vio was still with us and continued to be a such a help to me. We all liked her so much; Archie called her the "uncomparable" Vio. She was very devoted to Ian so we were never worried about leaving him with her when I went to the St. Augustine Club with Archie in the afternoons. Vio would bring Ian to the College grounds where all the college children used to collect and play and I expect the nurses all gossiped about their mistresses.

Ian was now nearly a year old and beginning to stand up and of course creep around the house. Archie and I were so happy together and Ian was such a joy to us. We all kept well and Archie liked his job at the College. Pyke, who had the same sort of job as Archie at the College, married Babs Jardine, a nice girl, and she had a little boy about Ian's age and she often came around to see me in the mornings and brought her little boy, Geoffrey, with her. Geoffrey and Ian took very little notice of each other. We would put them in the playpen and put a lot of toys in with them, which of course they proceeded to throw out of the playpen while Babs and I talked mostly about babies, what we fed them on, all the things they could do etc.

Pyke was one of the trio that worked together. Pyke and Pound worked in the Botany Department under Professor Cheesman, while Archie worked in the Chemistry Department under Professor Hardy. Unfortunately, Pyke got into someone's bad books and his contract wasn't renewed and he went out to Singapore, where we heard later that he was taken prisoner by the Japanese during World War II. He died there.

I felt so sad for them and thought of Babs who must have grieved so much for him, and being left with a little son and daughter. I never heard the full story of what happened but I expect Babs and the children were evacuated from Singapore and Pyke was left there. This is what happened to the English families in Singapore. I often thought that this may well have happened to Archie and I. I never saw Babs after they left Trinidad, but I know she and her two children lived in England. I suppose she received a pension or something. Just writing about her makes me sad.

Life continued happily for Archie and me. We had Vio who lived with us. She had a nice room outside and often bought her little girl Pearl to sleep with her at night. Pearl was about five years old. We also had a cook, but I can't remember a thing about her. She cooked for us and cleaned out the dining room, living room and pantry. Vio cleaned out our rooms and washed Ian's clothes and looked after him. We also had a washer woman who came with a tray on her head every Monday morning and took the dirty clothes and brought back the clean ones. They were always sparkling clean and beautifully ironed. I washed out my under garments and Archies' vests etc. I must say I really had an easy life and played a lot with Ian, supervised the house, sewed a little and read a lot. I often went into Port of Spain to spend the day with mother, daddy and Monica. Daddy would send Carrington in his car to bring me in.

At this time mother and daddy had moved from Belmont and took a house in Victoria Avenue near to the Government Printery. It was a nice house, big and roomy and very convenient. Mother wasn't very far from her family in Cipriani Boulevard and often went to see them and they often came to see her.

Daddy bought a radio (at this time radios were quite a new thing and it seemed wonderful that one could just turn a knob and get England or some other place, but was usually the BBC). The reception was nothing like it is today, but it was still very exciting to hear someone talking out of this little box and know that the voice was coming from England, and to hear Big Ben chiming the hours. I used to enjoy my days spent with mother, daddy and Monica. Monica was now becoming quite grown up and she was a very pretty girl with lots of admirers. I think at that time Fred Harragin was very much in love with her, but as time passes one forgets the exact sequence of events.

 *Pregnant Again*

IAN WAS ABOUT FOURTEEN MONTHS OLD when I got pregnant again. I was feeling very sick and knew that this would probably last for three months like it did when I was expecting Ian.

Well, this changed my way of life, my stomach felt upset and I couldn't do all the things that I used to do. Everyone speaks about 'morning sickness', but I was just as sick in the afternoons so didn't go to the St. Augustine Club for at least three months. I spent a lot of time with Ian and read a lot and just did a few things around the house. I liked going to mother and daddy's as I enjoyed the change of scenery and enjoyed the food more (even though I was often sick afterwards). During this period I ate a lot of Jacob crackers, which came in a tin and were fresh and crisp. I seemed to be able to keep them down much better than anything else. I suppose I should have been taking vitamins, but in those days no one took vitamins. I also ate a lot of fruit, and always had lovely sweet oranges and Portugal oranges that Vio used to peg out for me and gave me in a bowl.

As luck would have it, the same time I got pregnant, Vio got pregnant. She had a man friend called Joseph (I don't know his last name). He was a carpenter and was Pearl's father. Vio's one sorrow was that Joseph wouldn't marry her, his mother said that Vio was too dark (Joseph was much fairer than Vio—I think he had some Portuguese blood in him). Vio wasn't very dark, she was more brown and had a very pretty face, but she was a bit too fat. Vio wasn't at all ill when she got pregnant so continued to be a great help to me. I said to her "But Vio, what will I do when you have your baby and I have mine"? She said she would get someone who was good and would come back as soon as she could.

As with Ian, after the first three months had passed, I began to feel well and full of energy and had a very good appetite, but I soon began to get too big and had to think of getting some maternity things to wear, especially when I went to the St. Augustine Club in the afternoons.

Lorna Harragin Bryant had just had a baby girl, so she lent me her maternity dress. It was a nice dress, a navy blue with a big sort of cape which camouflaged my growing stomach. This was my uniform, with one other dress that I had when I was pregnant with Ian. I wore them both like a uniform. I hoped I would have a girl and then I would be quite satisfied with that as my family!

Dr. Gibbon was still our doctor and I went to see him and he said all was well. I didn't get Nurse Dottin again, she said she was getting too old now (I was very glad about this) so I engaged a black nurse called Nurse Frances. I can't remember who recommended her to me. She seemed very nice and I said I would like her to stay with me for two weeks, which she agreed to do.

Before I got pregnant, Archie's sister Melba came to stay with us, I don't remember much about what we did or what she did. She used to go to the St. Augustine Club with us and played tennis; we also had a big cocktail party for her and asked a lot of the young men that we knew at the College and some other young people, to tell the truth I don't remember much else about it. I remember Douglas Yearwood and Kit Wigley being there and I remember they asked Melba out and she met some other people and went to a few dances in Port of Spain.

When I was seven or eight months pregnant, the Duke and Duchess of Kent came to Trinidad to spend part of their honeymoon. Mr. Canning had a lovely house on a point on the mainland overlooking the sea (when one went down to Tetron Bay one could see it) and he lent it to them while they were in Trinidad. The Duke was Prince George, the brother of the King of England, and she was the former Princess Marina of Greece. There was a big reception for them at Government House given by the Governor of Trinidad (who was Sir Alfred Claud Hollis at the time). We were asked to the reception but I couldn't go as I was too big with the coming baby. Archie went and said it was a nice reception. He said he felt sorry for the Duke and Duchess who had to stand up and shake hands with all the guests. Then we saw in the papers that the Duke and Duchess of Kent were going to be driving around Port of Spain in an open car and one of the streets that they were going to be driving down was Cipriani Boulevard. So Archie said "Let's go down to Port of Spain and park in front of grandma's house and you can stand up in the car and put your head out of the sunshine roof and you will have a good view of them". So this is what we did and all the old people came, and so did mother and daddy and they stood near the car. I had a very good view of the Duke and Duchess as they drove very slowly down Cipriani Boulevard in an open car.

The Duchess of Kent looked very pretty and was beautifully dressed and the Duke of Kent was very handsome with the colouring of the royal family, very blue eyes, blonde hair and his cheeks were so rosy, they looked as if they had been painted! I was very glad to have had the opportunity of seeing them. The Duke of Kent was killed in a plane crash during World War II which must have been sad for his wife.

The time was now getting close for me to have my baby and I had everything organised, all the baby clothes etc. I had the beautiful crib that the Miss Dragos had given me, it was a real antique. The Miss Dragos had used that crib when they were babies. It really was a lovely gift and I don't think I appreciated it enough at the time. It was all mahogany and hadn't got a nail in it, the whole thing could be unscrewed and taken apart and just put together again. I used that one for Ian, and Ian's crib for the baby.

Birth of our Second Child

When I began to get pains, which started in the early hour of the morning on March 7th, Archie rang mother and daddy from a telephone at one of the College houses, as we had no telephone in our house, and Carrington brought up Nurse Frances. Mother and daddy came to be with me and they took Ian back with them to Victoria Avenue, at the same time Aunt Anna came to stay with me and help run the house.

Heather was born at about 4 o'clock in the afternoon. Archie had just come home from the office. I had asked him not to stay at home as he could not do anything to help me and I knew he was nearby at the College and I could get a message to him if I needed him. He had gone reluctantly but I knew how upset he would be if he stayed at home. When the baby was born Dr. Gibbon said "She is a lovely baby girl," and I looked over and saw Heather lying all wrapped up in a white towel with just her little head poking out and she looked so lovely with her eyes wide open, she seemed to be looking straight at me. I loved her with all my heart.

Until one's baby is born, one never realises how much one is going to love them. Suddenly I began to feel very weak and thought I was going to faint. I whispered to Nurse Frances that I was feeling very badly and I must have looked badly, as she ran to get Dr. Gibbon who was talking to Archie outside. Dr. Gibbon came quickly and gave me an injection. I don't know what it was, but in a short time I felt much better.

I was so glad to see Archie and show him our baby, whom by now the nurse had bathed and put in her crib. Archie was so relieved that the baby was born and all was well. We called our baby girl Heather, she weighed 9 lbs 2 ozs and was a lovely healthy baby. Nurse Frances was a very good nurse and looked after me and baby so well. Aunt Anna was so pleased to be with me and between herself and Nurse Frances they gave me very tasty meals. Heather was a good contented baby and in about four or five days I was feeling well and walking about and doing a few things. What a difference to when Ian was born and they kept me in bed for three weeks without getting up and I had gotten so weak.

With Ian (1936)

Mother and daddy came right away to see their new grandchild. They bought Ian with them but Ian wouldn't take any notice of the baby and didn't like to see me lying in bed. He said "Let's go grandma". I was very upset about this, but realised he was still very young and couldn't understand what was going on. The next time mother and daddy brought Ian to see me I was up and about and he was quite different but not at all interested in the new baby.

All this time Vio had been away as well and had her baby and it was a baby girl whom she called Pamela. Vio came to see me and said she was feeling quite well and would come back to me as soon as Nurse Frances left, but she would like to bring her baby, as she was nursing her. Mother kept Ian for me until Vio came back.

House on 1 Valleton Avenue, Maraval, which daddy called "Thelonica" (combination of his two daughters' names)

Archie, Ian, Thelma and Heather standing in driveway of Thelonica

Thelma's memoir ends with the birth of Heather, her second child. In the years that followed, she and Archie had four more children, all of whom were born and educated in the island of Trinidad, West Indies.

- Ian Archie, born April 18, 1933 in the house on the corner at the junction of Carmody and Pasea Roads, St. Augustine

- Heather Jacqueline, born March 7, 1935 at Circular Road, St. Augustine

- Gillian Mary, born January 30, 1939 at No. 6 Carmody Road, St. Augustine

- Robin Thelma Hilda, born February 24, 1943 at No. 1 Carmody Road, St. Augustine

- Monica Melba, born November 23, 1945 at Nurse Johnson's house, 1 Dere Street, Port of Spain

- Archie William Maclachlan, born December 27, 1952 at Nurse Johnson's house, 1 Dere Street, Port of Spain

Emmie, me, Heather and Ian in 1936 or 37 on the steps of "Thelonica"

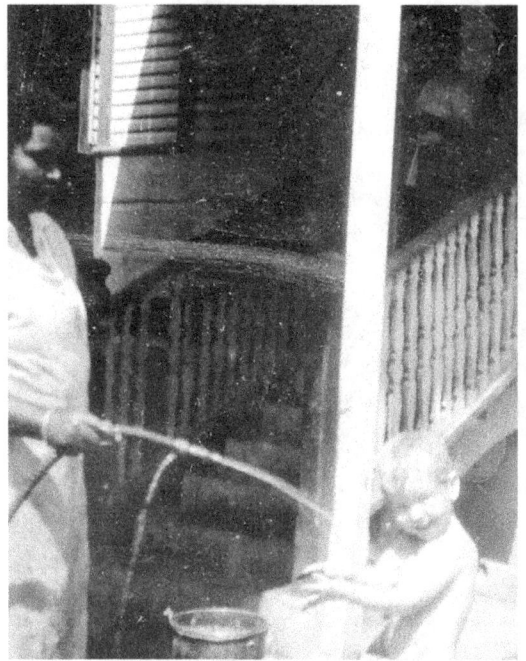

Vio giving Ian a bath (1935)

Vio holding Heather (1935)

Vio with Ian and Heather (1935)

*#1 Carmody Road, St. Augustine
when it was first built 1942*

While our children were growing up, we, Archie and I lived at No.1 Carmody Road, St. Augustine. In the year 1940 we bought one acre of land from Mr. Aikman who lived next door and had a 2 acre parcel. We paid $1,999 W.I. for the land, a good price in those days. We built the house in 1941. Gordon Grant & Co. Ltd. lent us the money. Mr. Geoffroy was the contractor and as we lived nearby, we watched the house growing before our eyes day by day. The construction was reinforced concrete downstairs and West Indian cedar wood upstairs. The final cost was $9,000 W.I. We moved in on January 2nd, 1942 when Ian was 9 years old. Heather was 7 and Gillian, 3 years. Robin was born at #1 Carmody Road the following year, in February 1943. This house was home to all our children.

*#1 Carmody Road 1962
On the lawn are Monica, Archie and Ian's son Keith*

*Cliff House when it was first built without wall (1947).
Prickly Pear Island is in the background.*

Postscript

With all their children grown and on their own, Thelma and Archie left Trinidad and settled in Archie's ancestral home in Antigua, where they lived for the rest of their lives. It was, and still is, a lovely home, built by Archie's mother Hilda McDonald in 1946/47 on a small bluff overlooking the beautiful Caribbean Sea (she called it Cliff House). It was her dream house and where she and husband, Dr. William (Willie) McDonald, lived for only a few years before her husband died. She left the house to Archie, her youngest son, and it is where the whole family, children and grandchildren have spent, and continue to spend, many happy vacations.

Thelma and Archie celebrated their 60th wedding anniversary on July 9th, 1992 at Cliff House, and it was the last time the entire family got together with them.

Archie died on August 6th, 1995 and Thelma, on March 7th, 1998.

Cliff House is home to Gillian Howie nee McDonald, Thelma and Archies daughter and her husband Doug, who recently passed away.

Right to left: Robin McDonald, Ian McDonald, Gillian Howie née McDonald, Heather Murray née McDonald, Archie, Archie jr. McDonald, Thelma, Monica Purkis née McDonald at Thelma's and Archie's 60th wedding anniversary (July 9, 1992)

Family reunion with children, spouses and grandchildren celebrating Thelma's and Archie's 60th wedding anniversary on seaside of Cliff House in Antigua.

Ian, Gillian, Robin, Archie jr, Monica and Heather at the gravesite of Thelma and Archie, buried at St. George's Church, Fitches Creek, Antigua, West Indies (March 1998)

 *Epilogue*
by her Children
Robin and Ian

Robin McDonald writes:

"My mother died in 1998, 2-1/2 years after my father, and it came to me to be the family archivist. There was an abundance of history on both sides of the family including a 'family history' and memoir written by my father as well as my mother, together with many other family treasures.

It was nearly 20 years ago that I first read mum's memoir, which she wrote down in three diaries. At the time, I knew I had to share it with my siblings and did so by typing it during lunch hours at work, had copies made and mailed off to them. I did the same with my father's memoir.

A few months ago, while going through family papers, I came across my mother's memoir and re-read it. This time, with 'new' eyes, I recognised my mother's voice, the 'matter of fact' way she spoke clearly came through to me, how much she loved her own parents, the deep love she had for her aunts and uncles, relatives and friends, and at times how fierce she could be when those she loved were hurt or bullied. In turn, later, when she became a mother, how much she and my father loved us. Most of all, the memoir confirmed the love, deep respect, and kindness they had for each other, which lies at the core of my own values.

Going through this process of getting our mother's memoir published has brought me closer to her, not only as my mother, but as a woman in her own right. I feel I have come to know her more intimately than when I was a young girl growing up. Perhaps it is because I left home at 19, returned to Trinidad to get married at 20, and then left again, making my home in Canada where I, my children and their families live. Although my family and I visited them often in Trinidad and then when they retired in Antigua, for the most part the relationship I had with my parents was from a distance, keeping in touch mostly through letters.

With the re-reading I also realised that this was not only my mother's story, but it was also the story of how life was for this particular young girl of French and British ancestry, and others like her of similar background born in early 20th century Trinidad, living all her life there until they retired to make their home in Antigua, settling in my father's ancestral home.

When I called Ian and told him how I felt after re-reading our mother's memoir, he listened and re-read the memoir himself, feeling as I did. He said he would look into how we could go about getting it into the hands of a publisher, which he did by connecting with Paria Publishing.

My mother was a country girl, born in Tacarigua, living in Brasso, Siparia, Tobago, Arima, St. Joseph, and finally settling down in Carmody Road, St. Augustine, first with her parents and then raising six of us at #1 Carmody Road. (sadly the house was turned into labs by the UWI, to be eventually torn down and as far as we know that piece of land is still vacant with just the old wrought iron gate and two beautiful samaan trees on either side remaining). My mother wrote this memoir for her children and grandchildren to have an account of what life was like when she was a girl growing up. It would never have dawned on her that what she had written would one day be published. Knowing this makes the memoir's publishing even more poignant.

The memoir also brought back my own memories as a little girl, of how loving my mother was, how quick to hug and throw her arms around us when we were hurt or ill, or just to tell us how clever, beautiful or handsome we were, and along with my father, so sure that we could be successful at anything we set out to do in life.

Many of the photos in this book were supplied by our cousins in the United States, particularly Ken, Michael and Trish Dale née Huggins, who are the children of Monica Huggins née Seheult, my mother's younger sister, as well as anecdotes from their mother's memoir. Ken Huggins in particular was of tremendous support, offering advice and scanning photos. Many of these photos neither I nor Ian had seen before. They have given me a window, not opened before, into the life of this extraordinary young girl and woman with her own dreams, who was to be my mother. I also came to know my mother's family through this process—my grandfather Leo, whom I never knew as he died before I was born, my grandmother Emmie, her sister Aunt Muriel and great-great Aunt Anna, all of whom I only vaguely remember, but have come to know and have a greater appreciation for through working on this project.

When I first re-read the memoir it also stimulated a nostalgia for the many exotic and beautiful places I explored as a child and young adult growing up in Trinidad, not only in St. Augustine where we lived, but other places. For instance, I was transported to 'Blue Basin' with its lovely waterfall surrounded by lush trees and rain forest sounds. Toco, and standing on the expanse of flat rocks below and surrounding the lighthouse, where the Atlantic Ocean and the Caribbean Sea meet as large waves topple over each other, the Atlantic Ocean rolling from the east and the Caribbean Sea from the west, and 'Blowholes' encased in the rocks around the lighthouse, gushing fountains of water with a roar, as rough seas bore down mercilessly against the hard surface, day after day, year after year. 'Bishop's House' where we stayed, that stood on top of a hill overlooking a grove of coconut trees through which we trekked down to the sea.

Then there were our holidays in Mayaro, its wide beach stretching for miles and miles, where the family dog 'Porky' would almost disappear into crab holes as he dug madly after a crab that had just scurried into it. Collecting chip-chips at low tide and putting them into a tin bucket with wet sand at the bottom so I could watch the little creatures peek out from their shell before burrowing a hole in hopes of escape. Poor things, I thought, soon cook would be making a type of callalou soup with them. Building sand castles and digging so deep we struck black oil sand that stained my feet and hands and I recall Mum saying, 'be careful, the tar will ruin your bathing suit'. At night, the kerosene lanterns casting shadows around the house, telling stories while listening to the waves lapping on the shore.

Macqueripe, Uncle Cory Davies and real American double-bubble gum. Las Cuevas, Maracas Bay, Point Baleine, Gasparee caves, Monos, the three Bocas;

rope bridges across the Caroni river, with the odd alligator basking on the muddy shore. The Caroni Swamp (now a great tourist attraction in Trinidad called 'The Trinidad Everglades') where, at sunset, the flight of Scarlet Ibis coming in to roost was breathtaking, they seemed to absorb the deep reds and mauves of the setting sun as they glided across the sky like clouds settling across the evening sky.

Remembering a walk through the Botanical Gardens in Port of Spain, with its ancient trees. We sat on their gnarled roots spread out over the ground like giant hands and rolled down the small inclines of the well-kept lawns that surrounded beds of beautiful tropical shrubs and flowers.

The giant samaan and jumbie bead trees in the I.C.T.A. grounds, so close to our home in Carmody Road, where I ran away many times to collect 'jumbie beads', and watch cricket and rugby matches. Climbing Mount El Tucuche and 'White Stone' next to Mount St. Benedict; cane fires at night lighting up the sky. The next day, donkey carts rumbling down Circular Road filled with succulent sugar cane, harvested from the fields, and running out of our yard, down Carmody Road, to grab one or two pieces that had fallen from the cart.

The list goes on, unleashing stories of another time, attached to each memory, each place. How fortunate we were growing up without the fears that exist for parents today in all areas of our world, not wanting their children too far out of their sight, or for too long, in fear of molesting or abduction. How fortunate to have had those freedoms to experience first hand the natural wonders of nature in a lush and lovely place like Trinidad. One wonders if adventures for our grandchildren will be virtual ones, experienced only through interactive computer games! A gloomy thought which I hope does not come to pass, but I fear it might, as the world becomes less inviting to embark on small adventures like the ones I, all my siblings, and my parents enjoyed.

*I*AN MCDONALD WRITES:

"My mother was very beautiful. I seem to have always known this—whether because to me, as a little boy, a mother of course was beautiful, or because as I grew up I heard people saying so and saw pictures and could compare her with great beauty, or because there was something wondrous in her which all men know as beautiful.

As I became older I kept this picture of my mother in my mind, so vivacious and pretty with red glints in her hair, and she told me a story once and I wrote a poem.

Beaucaillou

The wind blows my mother's thin grey hair;
she speaks of Beaucaillou, her swift horse.
When she was a girl she recalls
the fine horse in his gleaming trap:
the snort and stamp and jingle
and her father laughing, clapping,
shouting, 'Home, Beaucaillou, home!'
And the wind blowing in her red, wild hair.

When I was six I had been ailing and suddenly one day I felt a terrible pain in my gut. Dr. Littlepage was summoned and he examined me, and swung a gold watch on a gold chain to and fro I remember, and told my parents to take me immediately to the hospital and he would ring now for the surgeon to get ready. At the hospital though I begged they would not let my mother come into the operating room with me and I remember the tears falling from her eyes. They put the mask on my face and I knew they were going to kill me and I cried and shouted for my mother. When I woke up she was there. I had a raging thirst and I was desperate for water but it was not allowed. At last they let my mother touch my lips with chips of ice in a tablespoon and I looked into her eyes with unfathomable love. That night, I was told later, when they decreed she could not stay she said then they would have to drag her screaming out the room and even then she would fight her way back in. So they let her stay. Tears come into my eyes as I write. That night and the other nights she stayed with me and told me stories and sung me lullabies until I slept holding her hand—"golden slumber kiss your eyes."

Small memories caught in amber in the brain. I am hunting with my friends for butterflies in the hills near Mount St. Benedict Abbey. We are very thirsty and stop to see if we can get a drink. An old kind monk brings us water cooled in a big red jar. I see in a little shop pots of honey for sale and on the spur of the moment I buy one to bring home for my mother. I will not forget the look of delight in her eyes, the tasting of the honey right away, her lovely laugh of pleasure, the embrace that held me to her heart. Treasure from the Indies, I had brought for her.

When I was ten or eleven I began to play tennis seriously. My father had taught me the game and I soon became hooked. Weekends hot morning sun I would go to practise my shots against the green-painted wooden wall set up on one of the asphalt courts at the St. Augustine Recreation Club. Hour after hour I would play until I think I might have knocked a few boards loose. One day I came home badly sun-burnt and almost fainted. I nearly fell into my mother's arms. She was distressed beyond measure and rushed me to cool towels and rest in bed and wondered if a doctor should be called and was very sharp with my father for leading me into such goings-on. And when she saw I was fine again she scolded me very volubly and laid down the law it must never happen again. My father stayed judiciously quiet but later when the turbulent coast was clear he took me aside and told me how I must wear a big hat and lather sun screen on and take a big pitcher of iced lemonade with me—and I said I would for sure.

The two sides of the coin of their love which never failed to come up on the right side for me all my life. My dear parents, I see them now as if the light of those days shone again clear as ever.

There were times when our parents went partying at night. Our mother would come to tell us they were going. I must have been seventeen or eighteen because I remember in the room not only Heather, two years younger than me, but also Gillian, four years younger still and Robin, seven or eight—but not Monica "the baby" and not Archie who was born when I was at Cambridge.

Our mother would come in looking so beautiful in a fashionable, bright dress and take a few steps and spin around for us to see it twirl. "You are the prettiest in the world!" it is likely Gillie who exclaimed. And my mother laughed and bent to hug her and gave us all a kiss, "I love you!" And she would leave us happy, a vision of what it was to be radiant and joyous in the world. Our beautiful mother, our handsome father—we were proud of our parents.

Looking back, if I had to find one word to describe my mother it would be beloved. Beloved not to be misinterpreted as softly forgiving and sweetly loving always, the sugar of niceness ever-present. My mother had strong opinions and a sharp edge to how she expressed herself and flashes of temperament and a fine range of flares of temper when necessary. But those things and any faults she must have had, and nothing in her deep-down nature, impaired or detracted from the sense of her as one who was beloved. Something shone in her. There are such people.

Certainly I and all her children adored her unreservedly. Her mother—our grandmother Emmie—and great-Aunt Anna and Aunt Muriel all of whom were very close to us we could see loved her with a special, tender love. She gathered friends who were dear to her all her life. The people who worked for us in our house, Alice the cook, Vio one of many nannies, Ram the gardener—of those I myself remember best—worshipped her in her fundamental kindness. And I think of Willy Kong-Ting, for instance, who delivered groceries to our home on a bike when she helped give him a start in business and when he had become a supermarket magnate bowed down to her with tears in his eyes.

Above all, our wise and quiet father, her husband, her own beloved Archie, he knew she was born to be beloved and until the end of time—for sixty-three years and longer if you count from the time they must have fallen in love—he loved her forever. Yes, beloved, it is the word I think is best.

My mother told me she first set eyes on my father when she was a girl of twelve and she saw him after he had played a game of tennis and she fell in love with him on the spot. "Well, really, my darling mother," I teased her, "what were you doing eyeing up young men at twelve years of age!" She didn't mind, smiling and insisting that was how it was—though she admitted that she felt she didn't have any chance since girls five and six years older were lining up. But of course it turned out she did have a chance and the chance they both took ended up in a marriage which I their oldest child remembering all the years cannot think of being anything other than perfect. Therefore let me speak a little of their life-long love affair.

What relationship between human beings is the most complex, deep, intense? Passionate love between man and woman is surely a contender. For such love, men and women regularly surrender fame and fortune, comforts and distinctions, and sometimes even life itself. The tragic passion of Abelard and Heloise nine centuries ago astonishes and moves us still. Such love, it seems, has turned the course of history. Troy would not have burned but for such passion. Imperial Rome would have taken quite another direction had it not been for the mad infatuation of Antony and his Egyptian queen.

Perhaps deeper, more elemental, even than such passionate attachment is the parent-child relationship. What a mother, in particular, feels for her child predates reason and all ethics. It is encoded deeper than any scientist, philosopher or poet has ever explained.

And yet of all human bonds the most variable, volatile, and unclassifiable is the marriage bond. The relationship which grows between a man and a woman in a marriage is infinitely complex, mysterious in the extreme, subject to breakdown for a thousand reasons, yet immeasurably durable if the right, indefinable formula is found. A quiet, daily contentment is at the heart of most good marriages. As Nietzsche wrote, it is not the lack of love, but lack of friendship that makes unhappy marriages. Even the most passionate romances must evolve into friendship. And then you have a wonder of the world. A strong friendship within marriage is the most resilient, longest lasting relationship on earth. Weaknesses in both are understood, held always in perspective and forgiven. Strengths are shared and praised and therefore reinforced. Life's blessings counted day by day and shared are magnified, its burdens shared are lightened. Life's humour and its joys are never forgotten.

"No ill or wrong will overmaster this." It is not easy to explain, though in my parents I saw it all my life growing up. For them it lasted 65 years from first courting to the first death. It was love and companionship, but it was something more—a complete tolerance, affection, understanding, generosity towards one another. I always felt they had a foundation from which they could cope with anything—sickness, hardship, tragedy—a centred certainty turn and turn about in a world of ruthless change. Lord Longford, on his and Lady Longford's 60th wedding anniversary, was asked an obvious question and answered: "I never think about our marriage at all. It is rather like asking how I manage to breathe." Yes, it was something fundamental, something basically life-giving, like that.

No description or explanation can easily capture the essence. I suppose one can remember what Rainer Maria Rilke said about love—that it is a greeting between two solitudes. And then gradually, beyond greeting, beyond touching, those individual solitudes become one state that is solitude no longer and never will be again until death.

Deep in their retirement, I was visiting my parents at Cliff House in Hodges Bay, Antigua, where they lived in peace and beauty the last passage of their lives. Late evening we sat, the three of us, out on the rocks over-looking the blue-green sea turning dark with Prickly Pear Island in our view. Some late white gulls flew before nightfall screeching over the waves coming in eternally. In Guyana where I lived I had not been at all well but I was well again and I had come to see them. My mother asked me if I was eating enough. I hugged her and reassured her. My father gave a smile and a little shake of his head. I asked how things were going with them. They were happy but worried about children scattered far away out of reach of their love—except for Gillie and her Doug who lived with them at Cliff House and helped make life for them so good. They were hand in hand as we went inside, the stars big over Hodges Bay. I was close behind them. I looked at my old parents whom I loved so much all my life—as if they knew I said it they turned and smiled.

When my father died at the age of 89, my mother also began to die and gradually faded and diminished and disappeared in melancholy until two years later she joined him in death. We all shed tears remembering the joy and delight they had showed in each other for so long, how in perfect unison they had danced life's dance together.

The West Indian Club Ltd, incorporated in 1898 and active until the 1970s, was a gentlemen's social club. Its membership, made up of men from London, elsewhere in Britain, the West Indies and beyond, shared an interest in the West Indies. The club provided a social space for members, regular luncheons and dinners with invited speakers and guests, as well as promoted sports activities, including early cricket tours to and from the West Indies.
In this picture, Leo Seheult is captured in the middle behind the vase of flowers. This occasion was in honour of His Excellency Major Sir Hubert Young, K.C.M.G, D.S.O. Governor designate of Trinidad & Tobago, May 1935.

 *Notes*

Note 1: Leo Seheult. Leo was born at Santa Agua estate, Arima, Trinidad in 1885. He married Emily Gray in 1911. Leo was a Civil Engineer in the Public Works Department from 1909 to 1939 and Executive Engineer P.W.D. 1932-1939. He was the son of Adhemar Seheult, Civil Engineer. Born in Trinidad 1855. Married Louise de Maury de Lapeyrouse. Adhemar was the son of Jean Jacques Seheult, French Consul in Trinidad circa 1850, born in France. Married in Trinidad to Losia de Verteuil, daughter of Julien Michel de Verteuil who was the son of Jacques Alexis de Verteuil. Jacques Alexis de Verteuil and Louis Michel de Maury de Lapeyrouse were among the French Aristocrat families who fled from the terror of the French Revolution at the end of the 18th Century and came to reside in various islands of the West Indies, including Trinidad (Record by Archie McDonald).

Note 2: Carrington Oscar Thorington—we called him Carrington—was groom, waiter and yard-boy. He came to work for daddy when he was just a young boy and stayed with us until daddy died in 1939, living with us all those years.

Carrington had been with daddy as a stable boy before daddy married mother. He was a very handsome black man and really quite a man with the ladies.

"He had a gold tooth in the front and wore gold-rimmed glasses that he certainly didn't need for his eyesight. They were a status symbol and very effective with the ladies and the other chauffeurs. He was also our butler and a very good one. I don't know if it was mother's training or his pride in his job that made him put on the most precise English accent and dignified manner whenever we had company. The more important the company the more correct Carrington would be. You could always tell when he didn't think much of our visitors – he wouldn't even bother to put on his glasses if he didn't approve of them." (Monica Huggins née Seheult)

Note 3: Valenciennes lace A type of bobbin lace that originated in Valenciennes in the north of France, and flourished from about 1705 to 1780. Later production moved to Belgium in and around Ypres. The industry continued on into the 19th century on a diminished scale. (Source: Wikipedia)

Note 4: Description of Bertie Harragin and Leo Seheult (Thelma's father)

"Daddy was a short, heavy-set man with a bald head from the age of 20, and Uncle Bertie Harragin was 6'2". They were the best of friends and tennis partners. They were known as Mutt and Jeff. At one disguise party, Uncle Bertie dressed as a nurse and in a contrived baby carriage, there was my daddy as the baby, complete with bonnet and bottle." (Monica Huggins née Seheult)

Short biography of Bertie Harragin: Bertie Harragin was an officer of the Government. He had a creditable and unblemished 31 years of service, starting his career as a Sub-Inspector of Police in 1905, becoming an Inspector in 1912 and attaining Senior Inspectorship in 1934 with the rank of Major, finally retiring two years later as Deputy Inspector General of the Trinidad Constabulary with the rank of Lieutenant-Colonel. He was awarded the King's Police Medal and Volunteer Decoration. As a soldier, he was honoured with the Distinguished Service Order Medial in 1915 for distinguished service, and much noted for his gallantry. As a fighter, he was second to none in bravery on the field of battle. He was also an excellent sportsman and cricketer. (Source 'Public Life and Sport—Jamaica, Grenada and Trinidad', 1941)

Note 5: The piece of lead was used as a door stop for the stable door. (Monica Huggins née Seheult)

Note 6: Description of Bubbles, Thelma's dog "Bubbles, our dog, had one short back leg that had been injured when he was hit by a car. Half of one ear was gone; a bullterrier had the other half. He was beautiful! He was the splitting image of the old Victor Record dog — the one with one black and one white eye." (Monica Huggins née Seheult)

Note 7: Scott's house and pool in Maracas Valley "The Scotts lived on the Maracas Road in an old rambling house on the hillside. The most interesting thing about it the chapel. Old Mr. Scott and his family were very devout Catholics and they had built a small chapel overlooking the river.

It was the most restful place. When you were inside you could hear the river flowing over the rocks and under the bridge. The breeze blowing through the bamboos made a whispering sound and the brilliant sunshine would filter through the trees against the stained glass windows of the chapel, letting in the softest light. It was a most peaceful place and as a child I loved to go there. To get to the pool, we would walk or ride our bikes about five miles from our house in St. Joseph and mostly uphill as Maracas is in the valley of the foothills of the Northern Range. But the roads were not crowded and they were well shaded by the abundant bamboo and other tropical trees.

Maracas River flowed between overhanging bamboo, right by the Scott's chapel, under a bridge and over some big boulders to the pool below. It formed a basin right under the boulders and the Scotts had built a small dam just around the next curve to make it deeper. Down from the house along a gently-sloping path between the cocoa trees, and you were there. Under the trees grew patches of moss and a few wild flowers. It was always shady there, the sun filtering through the bamboo and samaan trees. For a short distance along the bank was a pebbly sand bar where we usually had our lunch. Opposite the beach, across the basin, were ledges of rock with ferns, moss and anthurium lilies. We'd climb up the rocks and dive into the pool.

One day, an Emperor butterfly flew over while we were swimming. He was a huge fellow, about six inches across, and one of the boys decided he wanted him for his collection. We must have run miles trying to catch him. Thank goodness he got away. He was too beautiful to be pinned down to a bed of cotton under glass.

While we were swimming, a coloured man came walking down the river bank with a deer slung over his shoulder. He had shot him upstream somewhere and was taking him home. He laid the buck down on the bank of the river while he quenched his thirst and we all gathered around to look. To this day I can remember the look in those soft, velvety eyes. I've never cared for deer meat since." (Excerpt taken from Monica Huggins' née Seheult memoir)

Note 8: Archie's illness "It was a game of rugby that nearly finished me off, at least it was the starting point of a long bout of serious illness that was to plague me for the next two years. Near the end of the first term of the 1927-28 academic year, at the end of November 1928, I emerged from a game of rugby in Port of Spain with an injured back. I felt at the time that the injury was out of the ordinary as the pain was intense, but there was nothing to show externally but some superficial bruising and abrasions in the small of my back. However, a few days later I was running a temperature and passing blood in my urine. The I.C.T.A. doctor sent me to the Colonial Hospital in Port of Spain where I was looked at by Dr. Wupperman. When Dr. Wupperman heard that my father was a doctor in Antigua, he advised that I should go to Antigua as soon as possible as he thought I needed a specialist's attention. I travelled to Antigua feeling far from well and soon after arriving there I developed general septicaemia, or blood poisoning, a condition usually fatal in those days as there was no medication equivalent to antibiotics or even sulfa drugs. As a treatment of last resort, my father, in consultation with other Antiguan doctors, decided to try an injection intravenously of mercurochrome, in itself a drastic shock to the system. Dr. Wright, who was then the surgeon at the Holberton Hospital, gave me the injection and a second injection 48 hours later. I survived the injections and they knocked out the infection in a damaged kidney that was attacking me. My convalescence was slow, but by April of 1929 I was able to travel to England on a Harrison Boat (the Ingoma or Inanda, I don't remember which). My purpose of going to England was to see a specialist in kidney ailments. I do not remember the name of the specialist who attended me, I just remember that I was sent to Belfast, entered the hospital, and for a few days or perhaps a week or more, became a guinea pig for a lot of very unpleasant tests. I was then discharged and returned to the UK with a regimen of medications that involved various pills that made me feel terrible but must have been good for me, and my health and strength gradually improved." (Excerpt from his memoir)

Note 9: Birth of Ian: "I was chatting with Mum at lunch today, 22nd April 1986, and she was telling me about Ian's birth. That was 53 years ago. Mum and Dad lived in a house at the top of Carmody Road, St.Augustine, and in those days women usually had their babies at home. Old Dr. Gibbon delivered Ian. Ian was a big baby, nearly 10 pounds, and Mum had to have stitches after the birth. Dr. Gibbon told Mum he'd stitch right away and she had eight stitches. Then Dr. Gibbon tied each of Mum's legs to a bedpost (the bed was a four-poster) explaining that the stitches would heal better if she could not move around. After lying flat on her back for a couple of hours Mum began to feel very uncomfortable. She complained to Nurse Dottin that she would not be able to sleep like this and the nurse told her that as soon as Dr. Gibbon went home she would untie Mum's legs but she was to be very careful how she turned in bed. Mum said, "What a relief that was"!

Mum said it was so hard to enjoy her first baby. Nurse Dottin told her that he had to be breast-fed every three hours on the dot and the three hours must be counted from the exact time she had finished feeding him until the time she started again. Then the worry was that the baby was getting enough milk. Nurse Dottin said the only way to know this was to weigh the baby after each feed. Sometimes he'd put on one ounce, but there was panic if he'd only put on quarter of an ounce.

The next thing was Mum had been given a lot of baby books telling her exactly how a baby must be brought up from birth to its best advantage. Mum wanted only the best for her baby so she was determined to follow the books exactly. One of the big rules was that you must not pick up your baby too often, certainly not every time he cried; usually only to feed and change him and for other certain reasons. Mum said she used to stand by the door looking at her baby waving his arms and legs in the air and screaming his head off and she'd start to cry as well as she was desperately longing to hold him in her arms and cuddle him, but no—the book said this would make the baby too dependent on its mother in later years. Once the baby was fed and changed he should be put back into bed; you must cut out the silly cuddling and fussing. Grandma Emmy Seheult (Mum's Mum) told Mum off about this and said it was all nonsense; she had always picked up her babies when they cried; but Mum argued that Gran was being old fashioned and the modern way must be better as it would help the baby grow into an independent, self-adjusted individual.

Mum said this lasted for about three weeks by which time she was completely frustrated and depressed and suddenly she couldn't stand it anymore, started picking up her baby and cuddling him, sitting in the rocking chair singing lullabies and saying little coo-coo things to him as he held her finger tightly in his hand and coo-cooed back. The books went into the wastepaper basket and Mum and baby were very happy from then on.

Mum had five more children and went on her own intuition for all the rest of us. We've all grown into well-adjusted human beings.

I remember Mum when she was in a warm, loving mood, holding her arms wide open and saying to whomever of us was there, "I love you all BIG SO" and giving us hugs and kisses." (Gillian Howie née McDonald)

Note 10: Lady Boats—The boats Thelma and Archie travelled on to Antigua and the UK in the 1930s From 1928 to 1952, interrupted only by World War II, Canadian National Steamships operated a fleet of five luxury liners, sailing from eastern Canadian ports to Bermuda, the West Indies, British Honduras and British Guyana, carrying thousands of passengers and millions of tons of freight. These immaculate white steamships offered a standard of service rarely experienced today.

Named after the wives of British admirals with a connection to the West Indies, the vessels were affectionately known as the "Lady Boats" and provided an efficient cargo service and romantic cruises for many years.

As sailing ships came to pass in the late 19th century, some of their routes were no longer profitable, and the Canadian government stepped in with financial assistance.

These vessels provided a year-round service every two weeks from Halifax to Bermuda, St. Kitts, Nevis, Antigua, Montserrat, Dominica, St. Lucia, Barbados, St. Vincent, Grenada, Trinidad and British Guyana before returning by the same route to Saint John, N.B.

A lot of attention was also paid to crewing and outfitting the Ladies. Experienced men were chosen as ships' captains and officers, instructed to see that the Lady Boats "had the same discipline and style as the large transatlantic liners."

Captains and senior officers were required to wear uniform frock coats on sailing and arrival days at the homeport, while dinner at sea was a full-dress affair. Ships' flags were raised and lowered daily in a formal ceremony.

Pursers were trained to rigorous standards, becoming known for their consideration and tact in handling customers, while the ships' Caribbean stewards were noted for looking after every detail of passengers' comfort.

A two-week cruise would normally cost $95 for a round trip. One season, offered a "honeymoon special" for only $85, which included Boston as a port of call.

She was the first Canadian merchant ship to go to war and helped enforce the blockade against occupied Europe. Shortly after entering service in her new role, she was sunk in the Bay of Biscay on July 16, 1941. But the war was about to move closer to home. (Excerpt from article by John Boileau from the *Legion Magazine* 2007)

Note 11: The Boat Archie McDonald travelled on to the UK in 1933 Either: INANDA 2. HARRISON LINE BOAT—1940 bombed and sunk in London Docks, repaired and renamed Empire Explorer for Ministry of Supply, managed by T & J. Harrison, 1942 torpedoed, shelled and sunk by U-Boat off Trinidad. INGOMA. 1915 (Source : www.The Shipslist.com)

Note 12: Ian Donald Roy McDonald was Archie McDonald's first cousin, after whom Thelma and Archie named their first child. Ian Donald Roy McDonald was the son of Donald McDonald, brother to Archie's father, Dr. Willie McDonald. IDR was born on the 9th September 1898 and enrolled at the Antigua Grammar School on the 6th May 1907 at the age of nine years. He spent six years at the AGS and having completed his secondary education there, traveled to England where he attended Denstone College, Staffordshire. Shortly after he joined the Royal Flying Corps at the age of seventeen.

Following welcome home address to IDR McDonald to Antigua dated August 1918 after his war service followed by his response:

"Captain McDonald: On behalf of the people of Antigua we beg to give you this heartiest of welcomes on your return for a short time to the land of your birth.

We are full of thankfulness that you have been so wonderfully preserved through numerous perils, and we recall with pride your splendid achievements in the battles of the air, and the distinction you have received from a grateful country.

We rejoice that a son of Antigua should have won such a remarkable record for bravery, skill and resourcefulness, and we look forward to further triumphs in a career which has begun so brilliantly.

We would include your father and mother in our welcome and congratulations, and we would assure them that we fully enter into their joy at your preservation from danger and at the honours you have gained. May God's blessing, guidance and protection be always granted you in the heroic life of peril and sacrifice to which you have pledged yourself.

Signed on behalf of the people of Antigua

" (Sd) A.P.Cowley
" R. Warneford
" Edwd. Bell
" R.S.D.Goodwin
" H.Y.Shepherd

Captain McDonald's reply was brief and direct but it conveyed the warmth and humility that radiated from this national hero anxious to share the tributes bestowed upon him and to identify with his West Indian heritage:

"Mr. Watkins, My Lord, Mr. Dean, Ladies and Gentlemen,

It is hard to find words to express the feelings I have for this tremendous reception you have given me. I can assure you that what I have done is nothing wonderful; I merely did what any other West Indian boy would have done – his best. When I go back I shall tell the others of the hearty welcome I have received and what they must look forward to when they come back. I must confess that I never expected anything like this and as I have never made a speech before I am afraid I don't know what to say. I thank you very much for this address and I shall prize it and keep it to be handed down."

His speech was given enthusiastic applause, and the band played a selection. "The Captain then shook hands with the members of the Defence Force, after which he and his father and mother entered into a waiting car. They then drove off for their home, the Bungalow, under an escort of the mounted volunteers amid the cheering of the crowd." (Excerpt taken from Antiguan historian E.T. Henry's 2004 essay on IDR.)

Captain Ian Donald Roy McDonald MC, DFC (1898–1920) (in picture with dog) was a British World War I flying ace credited with 20 aerial victories. Born in Antigua in 1898, he joined the Royal Flying Corps in 1916 and became a fighter pilot. On 26 April 1917, he was appointed a flying officer with the rank of temporary second lieutenant. He was first assigned to 39 (Home Defence) Squadron. From there, he transferred to A Flight, 24 Squadron on 11 July 1917. Flying an Airco DH.5, he scored his first three victories between 30 November and 10 December 1917. The squadron upgraded to Royal Aircraft Factory SE.5as. McDonald began to score with his new machine; his second victory on 26 February 1918, shared with Ronald T. Mark, Herbert Richardson, and three other pilots, made McDonald an ace. McDonald missed scoring in March, but was appointed as a flight commander with the rank of temporary captain on the 15th. He tallied six wins in April, four in May, and three in the first week in June. Then, on 17 June, teaming with Horace Barton, George Owen Johnson, and C. E. Walton, he forced down into captivity one of Germany's leading aces, Kurt Wüsthoff. He had become the squadron's second scoring ace. He exited the Royal Air Force in early 1919 and returned home to Antigua, suffering from eye strain. He then returned to the RAF, gaining a permanent commission as a lieutenant on 1 August 1919 and becoming an instructor at RAF Cranwell. In 1920, he was assigned to flight operations in Iraq. On 22 September 1920, he flew a DH.9a no. F2838 on a relief expedition to drop food to a stranded boat, the Greenfly. He was shot down by ground fire at Samawahon, and seen to wade ashore. He was executed at Dangatora. He is commemorated on Panels 43 and 64 of the Basra Memorial.

Jane Forward née Mc Donald, Hon. Donald McDonald and Mary McDonald and their son Capt. I.D.R. Mc Donald, with a friend leaving Buckingham Palace after receiving medals on 3rd July 1918.

Contemporary press statements:
Lt. (temp. Capt.) Ian Donald Roy McDonald, M.C.

A dashing, fighting pilot. In the past two months he has destroyed five enemy machines and brought down two others out of control. At all times he shows a fine offensive spirit and complete disregard of danger.

Supplement to the London Gazette, 3 August 1918 (30827/9201)

Lt. Ian Donald Roy McDonald, R.A.F.

For conspicuous gallantry and devotion to duty. With seven scouts he attacked eighteen enemy machines, of which three were destroyed and one driven down completely out of control. When driven down to within 200 feet of the ground by two enemy machines owing to a choked engine, he turned on them and drove one down. He has in all destroyed eleven enemy aircraft and carried out valuable work in attacking enemy troops on the ground.

Supplement to the London Gazette, 16 September 1918 (30901/10986)

www.ingramcontent.com/pod-product-compliance
Lightning Source LLC
Chambersburg PA
CBHW062108160426
42813CB00100B/2588